Chinese Characters

Han Jiantang provides an accessible, illustrated introduction to the fascinating history and development of the written Chinese language, from pictograms painted on rocks and pottery and ancient inscriptions to the refined art of calligraphy and the characters in use today. *Chinese Characters* will appeal to readers looking for an introduction to the rich but complex Chinese language, and to all those interested in the relationship between language and culture.

Introductions to Chinese Culture

The thirty volumes in the Introductions to Chinese Culture series provide accessible overviews of particular aspects of Chinese culture written by a noted expert in the field concerned. The topics covered range from architecture to archaeology, from mythology and music to martial arts. Each volume is lavishly illustrated in full color and will appeal to students requiring an introductory survey of the subject, as well as to more general readers.

Han Jiantang

CHINESE CHARACTERS

Translated by Wang Guozhen & Zhou Ling

CAMBRIDGE
UNIVERSITY PRESS

CAMBRIDGE
UNIVERSITY PRESS

University Printing House, Cambridge CB2 8BS, United Kingdom

One Liberty Plaza, 20th Floor, New York, NY 10006, USA

477 Williamstown Road, Port Melbourne, VIC 3207, Australia

314-321, 3rd Floor, Plot 3, Splendor Forum, Jasola District Centre, New Delhi - 110025, India

79 Anson Road, #06-04/06, Singapore 079906

Cambridge University Press is part of the University of Cambridge.

It furthers the University's mission by disseminating knowledge in the pursuit of education, learning and research at the highest international levels of excellence.

www.cambridge.org
Information on this title: www.cambridge.org/9780521186605

Originally published by China Intercontinental Press as
Chinese Characters (9787508513416) in 2009

This updated edition is published by Cambridge University Press
with the permission of China Intercontinental Press under
the China Book International programme ⟨⟩.

For more information on the China Book International programme, please visit
http://www.cbi.gov.cn/wisework/content/10005.html

First published 2012

A catalogue record for this publication is available from the British Library

ISBN 978-0-521-18660-5 Paperback

Contents

The Emergence of Written Language

Characters, regarded as a symbol of human civilization, first appeared in the East. Just as in the ancient pictographic languages of Sumer, Egypt and India, the characters of Chinese were first created in the form of "drawings." While those other languages have been lost in the course of history, Chinese has stood the test of time, and its characters remain in widespread use today.

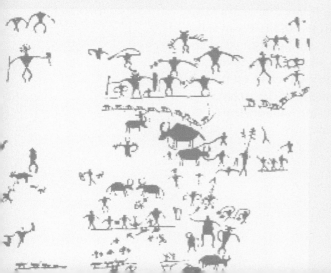

The Graphic Characters of River Civilizations

Characters are regarded as one of the most important symbols of human civilization, showing a progression from primitive to civilized society. The first known characters appeared in the early oriental "river civilizations."

The Journey to Civilization

Characters generally fall into two categories: pictographic and alphabetic. The oldest characters, created in ancient Oriental nations, fall into the pictographic category, because they evolved from drawings. About 5,500 years ago the Sumerians, who lived in the areas drained by the Tigris and Euphrates Rivers, invented cuneiform characters on clay tablets. Some 500 years later, the ancient Indians living in the Indus River valley invented characters of their own. Between 4,500 and 3,000 years ago, the Chinese people of the Yellow and Yangtze River valleys wrote characters on pottery, bone fragments and bronze utensils. These characters, all of which were pictographic, demonstrated the intelligence of the river people.

Symbols of Civilization: Characters are written symbols of language, and are amongst the most important symbols of human civilization. The development of language represented a great advance in human evolutionary history, and the emergence of a writing system for the Chinese language, in the form of characters, was also an important step forward.

The cuneiform characters on clay tablets in early times were pictographic symbols.

With the help of a brave little boy, H.C. Rawlinson, a British scholar, made rubbings of cuneiform characters on clay tablets, on the face of a steep cliff. It then took him at least twelve years to interpret the characters, eventually revealing the their secrets. As a result, Rawlinson earned his title "The Father of Cuneiform Characters on Clay Tablets."

Cuneiform Characters on Clay Tablets

Cuneiform characters are generally accepted as the earliest of their kind in the world. Created by the Sumerians in Mesopotamia some 5,500 years ago, Cuneiform symbols were impressed into clay tablets using reeds. Their strokes were thick at one end and thin at the other, giving the impression of a wedge or a nail. Known by later generations as "T-shaped characters," they were pictographic, having evolved from drawings. Although they were created by the Sumerians, they were very popular during the Babylonian period.

The Code of Hammurabi: The Code of Hammurabi was stipulated by King Hammurabi of ancient Babylon 3,900 years ago. The upper part is an exquisite figure engraving, and the lower part is the text of the code, inscribed onto clay tablets in 8,000 cuneiform characters. The code consists of 282 articles that clearly and comprehensively reveal aspects of social life at the time. The contents of the code show unequal policies regarding slaves and free men. For example, if a free man hit another and blinded him in one eye, one of his eyes would have to be blinded as a punishment; however if a slave owner blinded a free man, he would only need to pay compensation. If a slave owner blinded a slave, he would be protected by law and would not have to pay anything. The Code of Hammurabi made Babylon the most strictly controlled nation of ancient oriental times. It also greatly influenced legislation in other countries.

After about 3,000 years, however, the Cuneiform characters gradually died out. To date, some 2,000 years after their origin, they have been found on over 750,000 clay tablets, as well as on mountainsides, stone tablets, and pillars. The Cuneiform characters representing The Code of Hammurabi are thought to be the most spectacular of all, and were decoded by the British scholar H. C. Rawlinson, so that people could learn about ancient civilization in the two river valleys.

Stele of The Code of Hammurabi
The stele is 2.25m high. The engraving on the upper part illustrates the idea that "regality is granted by the gods." The seated Sun God is shown delivering a royal sceptre to the standing King Hammurabi. The lower part is the code, inscribed in 8,000 cuneiform characters onto clay tablets. The stele is now kept in the Louvre Museum in Paris, France.

Grave Symbols: Egyptian Pictographs

Some 5,000 years ago, ancient Egyptians living in the Nile River Valley created their own pictographs, and these can still be seen today on pyramids, stone objects, and pottery. The Egyptians inscribed pictographs onto papyrus, using reed pens, and bound them into rolls, which formed the world's first books.

In 525, when the Persians conquered Egypt, the Egyptian pictographs – which by then had existed for some 3,000 years – died out. The last person to understand Egyptian pictographs was a monk, and when he died their meaning was lost.

Pictographic Characters in Ancient Egypt

In 1799, when the French troops of Napoleon Bonaparte (1769–1821) made an expedition to Egypt, they discovered the Rosetta Stone, which was inscribed with ancient Egyptian characters. The characters were decoded in 1822 by the French scholar C. J. F. Champollion.

Mother River in Egypt – the Nile

Mysterious Seal Symbols: Ancient Indian Characters

Ancient India is regarded as one of the foundations of human civilization, because it made an important contribution to philosophy, literature, and the natural sciences. Ancient Indian civilization – specifically the Harappa Bronze Age Culture in the drainage areas of the Indus River - was re-discovered in the early twentieth century. The culture, which existed at around the same time as the Chinese Xia Dynasty (twenty-first to seventeenth century BC) began about 4,500 years ago, and disappeared quite suddenly some 800 years later. Archaeologists later discovered the ruins of several large cities, including Harappa itself, which became known as "The Manhattan of the Bronze Age." Characters from the Harappa period were discovered in the city's ruins. They were inscribed onto seals made of stone, pottery or ivory, and so were named the "Seal Characters." More than 2,500 seals and over 500 character symbols have been discovered, which consist mainly of pictographs, and some phonographs. Archaeologists were surprised to find such exquisitely detailed engravings of animals on each seal. Unlike the

"Seal Characters" in Ancient India
These mysterious symbols, engraved onto a small square seal, are clearly pictographic characters, whose mysteries are yet to be decoded.

The Indus River Running in Ancient Times

City Ruins of the Harappa Culture: the cities of the Harappa Culture, which have been discovered in the drainage area of the Indus River, are all very large. The houses were built from fired bricks, and systems were in place for water supply, drainage, and garbage disposal. Exquisite seal characters were discovered in the ruins of these cities.

Mesopotamian and Egyptian characters, the Seal Characters of ancient India have not been translated, so there is no known "Rosetta Stone" of Ancient India. The Harappa Culture also disappeared so suddenly, after existing for only a few hundred years, that the meaning of the Seal Characters remains a mystery to philologists and historians. The well-known ancient language Sanskrit emerged later on, and probably has no direct connection with the Seal Characters.

Engraved Words on Cattle Bones, used in Sacrificial Hunting

Han Characters: The World's Only Surviving Ancient Characters

China, one of the most ancient civilizations in the East, has a 5,000-year history of characters. The Han characters, created by the Chinese people, also originated from drawings and use pictographic forms to express meaning. Unlike the ancient characters of other civilizations, which have gradually disappeared, the Han characters have mysteriously endured. As a central aspect of Chinese culture, they continue to be used by generations of Chinese people, and have survived the changing dynasties almost unaltered. They are ideal for documenting the

The Yellow River running to the East

Chinese language, and have developed through the integration of form, pronunciation, and meaning, their meaning being expressed through their structure. The Han characters are the modern world's only existing descendents of the ancient characters.

The Origin of the Han Characters

The early Chinese people expressed meaning through drawings, and the Han characters are thought to have originated from these. Han characters are a form of ideographic visual symbol, and originated from the visions of the ancient Chinese people, as a particular way of representing the world. Amongst various legends about how they began is the popular story that Cang Jie, who had four eyes, created them.

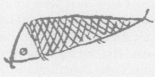

Legends in Ancient Times

Most mysterious ancient legends are said to have some basis in reality.

Fu Xi and the Eight Diagrams

A popular Chinese myth says that in the drainage area of the Yellow River in ancient times, an obscure figure named Fu Xi drew "Eight Diagrams," which became the origin of the Han characters. Fu Xi was a powerful emperor, and an important ancestor to the Chinese people. He was also very proactive, teaching people to make fishing nets and showing them how to feed livestock, so that they could earn a living from fishing, hunting, and animal husbandry. His mysterious Eight Diagrams were used for divination and are composed of the symbols "—" and "– –", "—" representing Yang, and "– –" representing Yin. Various combinations of Yin and Yang are arranged into eight groups of three. Each group represents a divinatory symbol with its own name, the names each representing different natural phenomena. The Eight Diagrams, however, bear very little resemblance to the Han characters, raising the question of how their basic long and short horizontal lines can actually have evolved into the Han characters' abundant strokes and complex structures. On careful observation it seems that only the numeral Han symbols are related to the eight diagrams. For example, the form

A Time of Legends: There are two great rivers in China, the Yellow River and the Yangtze River. Both flow relentlessly eastwards, bringing fertile soil to eastern China, where the ancient ancestors of the Chinese people first settled. They established a range of pursuits, such as fishing, hunting, gathering, farming, and the raising of livestock. This all took place in the Neolithic Age of primitive society, and represents the origin of Chinese civilization. It was a time of simplicity, but also of mystery and legend. Almost all of the traditional legends concerning the origin of the Han characters emerged during this period, about 7,000 to 4,000 years ago.

Mysterious Eight Diagrams

Fu Xi Temple
The Fu Xi Temple is situated in Tianshui City, Gansu Province. Fu Xi and Nu Wa, two important Chinese ancestors, are believed to have been born in this region.

of the number three "三" looks a bit like the figure of "乾(qián)" in the Eight Diagrams, "☰"; and the form of the ancient character for water (水) "⽔" bears some resemblance to the figure of "坎(ken)" in the Eight Diagrams, "☵". However on the whole, it is hard to see any close relationship between the forms of the other Han characters and the Eight Diagrams, making scholars sceptical as to whether they really originated from them.

Recording Events with Knots

Before the invention of characters, primitive people remembered important events in their lives by tying knots in ropes. For major events they would tie large knots, and for lesser events they would tie smaller knots. The more events there were, the more knots were tied. However only the people that tied the knots could understand their meaning, so although they helped in remembering events they could not function as a language, and it was impossible to create characters just by tying various forms of knots on lengths of rope. Academic researchers have suggested that some ancient numerical symbols evolved from knot symbols. The earliest developed Han characters are the Jiaguwen inscriptions, which were found on bones and tortoiseshells from the Shang Dynasty (seventeenth-eleventh century BC). Amongst these was the character "纪 ji" (meaning recording) which vividly illustrates of the act of recording. The period in which knots were used, was actually quite close to the time when characters started to evolve.

Picture of knots used for recording events in ancient times

Cang Jie and Characters: Astonishing the World and Frightening the Gods

One popular Chinese myth says that Cang Jie created the characters, a story that offers a valuable insight into their origin. More than 4,500 years ago, the Yellow Emperor, an important Chinese ancestor, united the areas drained by the Yellow River and established a vast community. Cang Jie was the Emperor's historiographer, and also a magician. It is believed that he could write characters almost from birth, and that he had four eyes, which meant that he could observe all the world's objects. He could raise his head to look at the forms of the stars, and he could lower his head to watch birds and animals on the ground. From this he observed that objects were distinguished by their different forms, and based on this he created pictographic characters. The legend says that through his characters, the secrets of Heaven

Image of Cang Jie, who is said to have had Four Eyes

and Earth were revealed, and that this frightened the gods and the ghosts, making the ghosts cry all night, and millet fall from the sky. The creation of the Han characters, then, was considered a major event that "astonished the world and frightened the gods," and so they had a very sacred meaning to the ancient people.

Today it is hard to believe that the Han characters were created solely by Cang Jie. The set of standardized characters that we see today, must have resulted from considerable development, and indeed, they were created collectively by the Chinese people over a long period of time.

The legend of Cang Jie, however, disclosed an important historical fact: Some 4,500 years ago, the Yellow Emperor united the areas drained by the Yellow River, and Chinese civilization was established. It is believed that the characters were first created during this period. Their creation is likely to have involved a considerable number of people, who would each have written in a different way, but the input of somebody like Cang Jie would have been needed to settle such differences, and to come up with a definitive character to

Picture of Cang Jie Creating Characters. It is believed that the creation of characters by Cang Jie astonished the world, and frightened the Gods and ghosts to the point of tears.

express each meaning. The most important fact that the legend tells us is that Han characters are a form of ideographic visual symbol, and that their genesis was in drawings.

Han Characters, said to have been written by Cang Jie

The Han Characters' Origin in Drawings

Calligraphy and paintings are said to have the same origin, and are likened to two brothers, albeit with a large difference in age. While characters have a history of 6,000 years at most, paintings can be traced back scores of thousands of years. Nothing expresses meaning more simply and directly than a drawing, and it was only after a long time that drawings became more abstract and symbolic, eventually evolving into characters that could be pronounced as speech.

Cangyuan Rock Paintings in Yunnan Province, China (from the Neolithic Age)

Recording Events with Simple and Unvarnished Rock Paintings

Rock paintings are the oldest known paintings in history. The earliest ones emerged about 20,000 to 30,000 years ago, engraved or painted onto cliffs by early humans, and represented everyday life in primitive society. The famous cave paintings in Altamira, Spain, and in Lascaux, France, and the rock paintings in Inner Mongolia, Qinghai, Yunnan, and Jiangsu, China, all vividly illustrate the ancient and mysterious primitive world. These old drawings, created before the invention of characters, were used to record events. Rock paintings used artistic forms to express a narrow range of meanings. They had no relation to language and no spoken equivalent, so they were not characters; however they recorded

Yangshao Culture: The culture associated with the areas drained by the Yellow River dates back to the Neolithic Age, and has a history of 5,500 to 7,000 years. By that time, people had settled into established lives, and millet was a major agricultural product. Other common pursuits included fishing, hunting, and the painting of pottery. The Yangshao Culture is so called because it was discovered at Yangshao Village, Mianchi County, Henan Province. Pottery from the Yangshao Culture contains many vibrant ideographic drawings, which must have had a role in the creation of pictographic characters. Some earthenware from the era was carved and painted with geometric symbols, which are also related to the Han characters' development.

Ancient Rock-Paintings in China
Many rock-paintings developed into specific patterns and looked similar to pictographic characters. The drawings in the painting could be the original forms of pictographic characters such as 牛Niu (cattle), 犬Quan (dog), 牧Mu (herding), 鸟Niao (bird), 人Ren (people), 射She (shooting), 亦Yi (armpit), 舞Wu (dancing), 美Mei (beauty), 女Nu (female), 面Mian (face), 日Ri (sun), 木Mu (wood), and 车Che (vehicle).

events by illustrating natural things and human activities, and expressed meaning visually, so they had a similar function to characters. It is worth mentioning that some ancient rock paintings in China contained patterns and symbols, and others were similar to the pictographic characters of later times, so rock paintings must definitely have played a role in the subsequent formation of pictographic characters. Therefore, although we cannot say that the rock paintings themselves were characters, we can infer that they were a source for them.

Exquisite Decorations on Painted Pottery

Pottery is a symbol of the Neolithic age, and China was one of the first ancient civilizations to understand how to make it. During the age of the Yangshao Culture, a range of drawings and decorative patterns were painted onto earthenware in the areas drained by the Yellow River. They were simple and unvarnished, yet vivid, interesting, and very decorative, demonstrating our ancient ancestors' artistic skills. As the patterns on them were coloured, the earthenware items became known as "painted pottery." They were most prominent in the period of the Yangshao Culture, which is often referred to as the "culture of painted pottery." These artistic images, however, were intended only for decorating pottery, and did not form symbols, nor were they related to language, pronunciation, or the communication of information, so while they were excellent works of art, they were simply drawings, and not characters. Nevertheless, some of the drawings did take the form of ideograms, and thus paved the way for the creation of pictographic characters.

Colored Pottery Urn from the Majiayao Culture
The Majiayao Culture is also known as "Gansu Yangshao Culture." The surfaces of its colored pottery urns are painted with Moire and patterns of curly grain. This clearly represents the daily life of the people who labored and raised families in the area drained by the Yellow River, some 5,000 years ago.

Two Kinds of Pottery Carving and Symbol Painting

In ancient times the Chinese people carved and painted symbols onto pottery. These had a

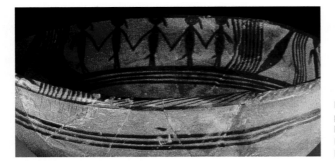

Pattern of people dancing, painted onto a painted pottery basin in Majiaoyao Kiln, Gansu Province (Yangshao Culture Period)

significant relationship with the Han characters, and are important data for research into their origin. The symbols principally fall into two types: geometric symbols and image symbols.

Shaanxi Province. In the ruins of the Yangshao Culture in the middle reaches of the Yellow River, and specifically in Banpo Village and Jiangzhai Village in Xi'an, Shaanxi Province, archaeologists discovered many earthenware items with geometric symbols on them. These symbols, which consist of lines carved and painted onto pottery about 5,000 to 6,000 years ago, are so simple and abstract that it is difficult to decipher their meaning, or to identify them undoubtedly as Han characters. However, many of

Dawenkou Culture: This culture dates back to the Neolithic Age, and has a history of 4,500 to 6,000 years. It is mainly associated with Shandong at the lower reaches of the Yellow River, and the northern parts of Jiangsu and Anhui. In ancient times the culture had a maternal clan commune system, which later developed into a paternal clan commune society. At that time, farming had become a major form of livelihood, and the production of pottery had also flourished. Dawenkou earthenware was both white and black, and some was carved and painted with image symbols. These symbols might well have been the earliest characters in China.

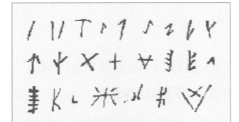

Symbols carved and painted on pottery, unearthed in Banpo, Xi'an

Symbols carved and painted on pottery, unearthed in Erlitou

them were repeated, which suggests that they were created with serious intent, and so must have functioned to record events. It should be mentioned that these symbols did influence the creation of Han characters in later times, and some may well have originated from them.

The ruins of the capital of the first Chinese dynasty, the Xia Dynasty (twenty-first–seventeenth century BC), were discovered in Erlitou, Henaan Province – one of the greatest archaeological discoveries of recent times. More than 20 different types of carved and painted symbols were found on pottery, which dated back at least 4,000 years. The forms of the symbols were very similar to those found on the earthenware excavated from Banpo and Jiangzhai villages, and some of them were very similar to the Jiaguwen inscriptions of the Shang (seventeenth–eleventh century BC) and Zhou (eleventh century-256 BC) Dynasties. We cannot say for certain that those geometric symbols were characters, although the structure of their lines was notably consistent with them. We can say, however, that the Han characters are likely to have originated from the symbols carved onto the pottery of the Yangshao Culture.

Image Symbols. Image symbols, which use lines to describe objects, displayed obvious differences from geometric symbols, and are similar to the Jiaguwen inscriptions that were found on bones and tortoiseshells from later times. The same symbols have

The sun rising over the Taishan Mountain
The Dawenkou people in ancient times often witnessed this beautiful sunrise.

been found in many places, which implies not only that they were used for communicating information, but also that they were in frequent use, and might have had a corresponding pronunciation. Because they seemed to have form, meaning, and pronunciation, experts believe that the symbols carved and painted during the Dawenkou Culture should be recognized as the earliest characters in China: the original image characters.

The picture to the left shows a symbol carved onto earthenware. This symbol can be found in several different places and looks like a drawing representing the morning, with the sun rising over the mountains, piercing through the clouds, and gradually illuminating the world below. Many philologists believe that this is the character of "旦 dan" (meaning dawn), and others believe it could be "昊 hao", "盟 meng", "炅 jiong", or "炅山 Jiongshan Mountain". The upper part "日" illustrates the sun, and the lower part "—", is a simplified illustration of mountains and clouds. We cannot say for certain whether the symbol "旦" carved onto earthenware

Pottery from the Dawenkou Culture, with the Symbol of "旦.Dan" Carved onto it

really represents the sunrise over the Taishan Mountains, but it is feasible. Many philologists think the symbol "旦" was a clan totem, which is also possible, because according to studies of the Han characters, many clan totems or emblems were incorporated into them in later times.

The Time of the Han Characters' Origin

The geometric symbols painted onto ancient pottery were formed of lines, and the image symbols were ideograms. These were important features of the developed Han characters that would later appear in the form of Jiaguwen inscriptions on bones and tortoiseshells. The symbols found on ancient earthenware, then, are likely to be the origin of the Han characters. Of these, the image symbols had the closest relationship to them, and so might be their direct ancestor. If we link this to what we know about the Han characters' history, we can trace them back to the period of the Yangshao Culture, approximately 6,000 years ago. The earliest known group of Han Characters are said to have appeared in

Philologists believe that these totems or clan emblems on pottery and bronze ware are the origins of pictographic characters such as "蛇She (snake)", "象Xiang (elephant)", "猪Zhu (pig)", "牛Niu (cattle)", "龙Long (dragon)", "虎Hu (tiger)", "犬Quan (dog)", "羊Yang (sheep)", "鹿Lu (deer)", "鸟Niao (bird)", "鱼Yu (fish)", "月Yue (moon)", "日Ri (sun)", "山Shan (mountain)", "火Huo (fire)", and "美Mei (beauty)".

the Taishan Mountain region about 4,500 years ago, but further excavations are needed in order to confirm this.

In the meantime, the symbols found on the earthenware of the Dawenkou Culture, though considered to be early Han characters, were still more similar to drawings. There were also far fewer of them than there are in the Han character system, so it is not easy to ascertain their historical connection to them. More than 1,000 years later, characters emerged that were comparatively more developed, such as the Jiaguwen inscriptions, which indicated the phase of the "ancient characters."

The Evolution of the Han Characters' Forms

The Han characters evolved over a very long period. The Jiaguwen inscriptions on bones and tortoiseshells from the Shang Dynasty are the earliest examples of developed Han characters. In the 3,000 years that have passed since then, the Han characters' forms have evolved through Jiaguwen, Jinwen (inscriptions on ancient bronze ware), Xiaozhuan (the lesser seal style Chinese characters of the Qin Dynasty (221–206 BC), Lishu (the official script of the Han Dynasty (206 BC–220 AD), and Kasha (regular script). Drawings have gradually evolved into strokes, pictographic characters have become symbols, and complex characters have become simplified. Simplification has been a central process in the development of the Han characters.

Ancient Drawing-like Characters

We have never been able to find out as much as we would like about the first Chinese dynasty, the Xia Dynasty (twenty-first to twenty-seventh century BC), and some scholars are even doubtful that it ever happened. But we know comparatively more about the second dynasty, the Shang Dynasty (seventeenth-eleventh century BC), thanks to the Jiaguwen inscriptions found on bones and tortoiseshells from the era. If Sima Qian, a historian from the Western Han Dynasty (206 BC- 25 AD) had been as knowledgeable as we are today, his famous book *Shi Ji (Historical Records)* would have been even more influential in this respect.

Characters from Underground: Jiaguwen

A Time of True History:
After the stage of the "primitive drawing characters," the Han characters entered a new phase of "ancient characters." These characters still looked like drawings to some degree, but were comparatively mature, and were represented in Jiaguwen, Jinwen and Xiaozhuan. These more developed Han characters indicated that China had progressed from a time only recorded in folklore and legend, to a genuine historical era.

The Jiaguwen inscriptions, found on bones and tortoiseshells from the Shang Dynasty, are a fascinating type of writing. Their creation was related to the gods and ghost-worshipping rituals of the dynasty, and their excavation after 3,000 years is a fascinating story in itself. Some 100 years ago, local farmers working in the fields of Xiaotun Village, Ayang, Henan Province, found fragments of bone in the soil. They converted them into a traditional Chinese medicine called "longgu" (dragon bones), and sold them to pharmacies for extra income. The "dragon bones" were actually Jiagu bones, and the symbols on them – thus known as Jiaguwen inscriptions - had been hidden underground for over 3,000 years. Jiaguwen characters originated in the Shang and Zhou (eleventh century-256 BC) Dynasties, and represented an integration of form, pronunciation, and meaning.

They were used to record each word in spoken language, had pronunciation, and were arranged into phrases and simple sentences. Jiaguwen was an ideographic symbolic language, that was both spoken and used to record complex ideas, and consisted of quite developed characters. Scholars consider it a tragedy that for so long its inscriptions were ground up and taken as medicine.

A Discovery from Traditional Chinese Medicine. The Jiaguwen inscriptions were first discovered in 1899, when an official named Wang Yirong, who was in charge of wine sacrifice at the Imperial College of the Qing Dynasty (1644-1911), fell ill and bought some "dragon bone" medicine from Beijing Darentang Pharmacy. An educated man who was already fond of characters, he studied the bones and realized he was looking at the ancient characters of the Shang Dynasty. As they were inscribed onto tortoiseshells and bones, the people of later generations came to call them "Jiaguwen." The region around Xiaotun Village, where the bones had come from, had once been the capital of the Shang Dynasty, called "Yin." After the fall of the dynasty, the area had gradually fallen into ruin and eventually been

A piece of tortoiseshell containing inscriptions from the Shang Dynasty (17th - 11th Century BC)

Some 150,000 pieces of animal bone and tortoiseshell have been unearthed from Xiaotun Village, Anyang (The Ruins of Yin).

Jiaguwen characters with thin, rigid and straight lines inscribed onto cattle bones from the Shang Dynasty (17th-11th Century BC)

Yin's Ruins: The ruins of the Yin, located in what we now know as Xiaotun Village, Anyang, Henan Province, was the capital of the Shang Dynasty, 3,000 years ago. It was also the earliest settled capital in China's history. In 1300 BC the twentieth king of the Shang Dynasty, Pan Geng, moved the capital to Yin, where it remained until the dynasty's end. More than 80 palaces and ancestral temple ruins, as well as 14 grand imperial graves, have been excavated from Yin's Ruins, along with many cultural relics from the Shang Dynasty, including examples of Jiaguwen, bronze ware, jade, pottery, ornamental stone, lacquer ware, and textiles. In total, more than 100,000 pieces of Jiaguwen have been discovered. In July 2006 Yin's ruins were added to the list of World Cultural Heritages. The international examination panel compared Yin's outstanding historical value to that of Egypt, Babylon, and India.

submerged, and was referred to as "Yinxu," meaning "the ruins of the Yin." After Yirong's discovery, farmers dug hundreds of thousands of Jiaguwen pieces from the ruins, and since then, over 150,000 pieces of Jiaguwen from the later Shang Dynasty and Western Zhou Dynasty (eleventh Century - 771 BC) have been unearthed from Yinxu and other places. More than 4,500 characters have been discovered, and more than 1,500 of them have been interpreted.

Mysterious divination. Why did the people of the Shang Dynasty inscribe characters onto tortoiseshells and animal bones? Their culture was spiritual and superstitious, worshipping gods and ghosts, and the emperor of the dynasty would use the bones and tortoiseshells to ask the gods questions, such as whether there would be a harvest, how strong the wind and rain would be, and whether or not they would be victorious in war, or successful in hunting. Believing that the gods would give them the answers, the emperor's officials would make small round holes on the backs of the shells and bones, using a red-hot bronze stick, and then call on the gods to answer the emperor's questions. The heat would then cause the shells and bones to crack, and the nature of the crack – whether it formed on the upper or lower side – would determine whether the gods' answer was positive or negative. If it was positive, the people could go ahead with the activity in question, and if negative, they would have to refrain. The officials would inscribe the result onto the shells and bones, forming the Jiaguwen inscriptions. Jiaguwen inscriptions, then, are considered sacred, having been a means of communication between man and god. Some Jiaguwen pieces were also used for recording events.

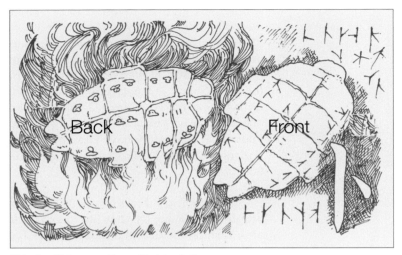

Divination Picture on a Burned Tortoiseshell

Vigorous Line Drawings. The characters of the Jiaguwen inscriptions had various forms, such as pictographic, directive, associative-compound, and pictophonetic. Jiaguwen was an ancient character language with its basis in drawings. Its pictographic characters represented the typical features of objects; for example the characters "(鹿) deer" and "(虎) tiger," though drawn in different ways, all show horns and stripes. In Jiaguwen the character "(马) horse" shows the mane on the horse's neck. The basic structure of a Jiaguwen character was composed of lines and strokes. Because bones and tortoiseshells are hard, it was difficult to write on them, so the Jiaguwen strokes consisted mostly of straight lines, carved using the point of a knife. The lines were thin, rigid, and straight, and the curves were mostly square, displaying primitive simplicity. As part of an early writing system, Jiaguwen characters were in some respects immature; for example they were inconsistent in size and in the way they were written, the number of strokes used for each character would vary, their components did not have fixed positions, and there were many "combined characters," made up of two or three characters. As Jiaguwen characters were prominently pictographic and ideographic,

Tortoiseshell from the Shang Dynasty, inscribed with a Divination Passage (detail)

Tortoiseshell Divination in the Shang Dynasty: A complete divination passage on tortoiseshells and animal bones should include the time of the divination, the people, things and reasons involved, and the results and verification. As there was so much content, it had to be inscribed onto pieces of tortoiseshell, and the amount of writing had to be small. Therefore the written language of ancient China is characterized by its brevity, which bears a direct relation to tortoiseshell divination. At that time, tortoise shells were used mainly as tools for divination in the court of the Shang Dynasty. According to the ancient folklore, the world was carried on the back of four heavenly tortoises, and their shells were printed with the mysteries of Heaven, and their undersides with the mysteries of Earth. Because tortoises were considered sacred, people believed that they were more accurate than animal bones terms of forecasting. Tortoiseshell divination prevailed during the Shang Dynasty.

ordinary people could still recognize them, even at such an early stage in their development.

Jiaguwen characters - drawings composed of lines - were indicative symbols whose meanings people could understand, which suggests that they were in the process of development towards more mature, linear characters. The large number of ideographic divination words on tortoiseshells and animal bones tell us that as early as the Shang Dynasty, over 3,000 years ago, Han characters had become a relatively complete system for recording language.

History and Culture. Jiaguwen inscriptions on animal bones and tortoiseshells have provided us with a wealth of authentic information about the Shang and Western Zhou Dynasties, and have become the most reliable data on which we can base studies of those eras. For example the famous divination words on cattle bones, "Multitude Working on Fields," from the Shang Dynasty, tell the story of the emperor of the dynasty asking the Heavens, "if the emperor orders lots of people to work together in the fields, will we have a good harvest?" These characters reflect the fact that farming in the Shang Dynasty was conducted by slaves in groups. "The Moon Eclipse Again" – a set of characters carved onto cattle bones from the Shang Dynasty – also have a great scientific value. They have been interpreted as meaning "Renyin

Typical examples of Jiaguwen inscriptions on bones or tortoiseshells

Zhen Moon Eclipse Again (壬寅贞月又食) – Renyin indicating the year, and Zhen meaning divination – and are said to be the first written record of a full lunar eclipse, which occurred on 2 July 1173 BC. The same eclipse is also recorded on another piece of cattle bone from the Shang Dynasty, "Record of Solar Eclipse." The record in Jiaguwen of Fuo Hao, a female general of the Shang Dynasty, also provides a vivid account of the era.

Famous cattle-bone inscribed with characters relating to "Multitude Working in Fields" (from the Later Period of the Shang Dynasty, Excavated from Xiaotun Village, Anyang, Henan Province)

Famous cattle-bone telling the story of "Moon Eclipse Again" from the Shang Dynasty, Unearthed from Xiaotun Village, Anyang, Henan Province

Fu Hao, the brave and beautiful female general of the Shang Dynasty

The Mystery of Fuo Hao. In 1976, archaeologists excavated a large grave from the Shang Dynasty, in the palace area of Xiaotun Village, Anyang, and found almost 2,000 pieces of bronze and jade objects buried alongside the corpse. The body was that of a woman named Fu Hao. There was no record in any ancient book of who she was, but the archaeologists were very excited to have found her, as her name had already appeared frequently in Jiaguwen, on over 200 pieces of tortoiseshell and animal bone. The excavation revealed her to be the wife of Wu Din, an emperor of the Shang Dynasty, and a brave and beautiful female general. She held many sacrificial and religious ceremonies at the palace, and was regarded a prestigious figure. The inscriptions tell her bittersweet story. Wu Ding loved his wife passionately. She was well versed in both letters and the martial arts, and after she returned from battle, Wu Ding would meet her on the outskirts of the town, where they would hunt together and capture deer. Wu Ding was constantly concerned about Fu Hao's welfare, as the battle was still raging outside the castle walls, and every day he would ask the gods questions about her, such as "it's raining in the north; will she get wet?", "will she be careful?", "will she be cold?", and "she is in pain – will she be o.k.?" The short-verse words of divination found on the animal bones inscribed by Wu Ding, all expressed his profound thoughts on, and endless love for, Fu Hao. Fu Hao died at the age of 33, and Wu Ding was consumed with grief. After a ceremonial funeral, he buried his beloved wife within the palace walls. The Jiaguwen characters revealed the story of Fu Hao, a touching and sad love story from the Shang Dynasty.

Characters representing "Fu Hao (妇好)", which frequently appeared on tortoiseshells

The Wonder of World Bronze Ware Culture: Inscriptions on Bronze

In about 3,500 BC, the East entered the Bronze Age. The earliest bronze ware of the era appeared in Mesopotamia and Egypt, and the Chinese "Age of Bronze Ware" emerged a little later, in about 3,000 BC. During the era of slavery in the Shang and Zhou Dynasties, the Chinese Bronze Age reached its peak. Through artistic shapes, exquisite line decorations, skilled craftsmanship, and majestic inscriptions, it became a wonder of the contemporary world. Bronze ware was formed mainly of bronze with some tin, and had a polished sheen. At the time it was called "Jin," so the inscriptions on bronze ware items were known as "Jinwen" ("wen" meaning "inscriptions"). The highest sacrificial bronze vessels were ding (tripods) and zhong (bells), and were represented by the most characters. These characters were known as "Zhong Ding Weng." A large number of inscriptions appeared on Chinese bronze ware, and remain of great interest to historians of the Bronze Age.

Bronze *zun* painted with exquisite and brilliant decorative lines from the Shang Dynasty (17th-11th Century BC)

Sacrificial Vessels Buried Underground

Bronze ware was considered precious in the Shang and Zhou Dynasties. Bronze items were sometimes used as containers, but they were mainly used as sacrificial objects, offered by nobles and slave owners to their ancestors and the gods. At the time, bronze ware had become a symbol of power and prestige, and people in the highest societal positions possessed the most bronze ware. The bronze ding tripod, for example, was one of the most important sacrificial items in the country. A king would have the most pieces – around nine - and nobles would have between one and three, whereas ordinary people could not afford any. At the time, princes and nobles would inscribe great events such as sacrifices, battle victories, awards, and slave trades onto their bronze ware, for permanent preservation. The style of Jinwen was similar to that of the Jiaguwen inscriptions. After the death of a prince or

An inscribed Simuwu Bronze ding from the Shang Dynasty

noble, their bronze ware would be buried with them. Almost all of the bronze ware from the Shang and Zhou dynasties that we see today, has been excavated from burial sites.

Majestic Jinwen. The bronze ware of the Shang and Zhou Dynasties started to be unearthed as early as the Han Dynasty (206 BC – 220 AD), and since then tens of thousands of items have been excavated. More than 3,000 different Jinwen characters have been discovered on them, and more than 2,000 have been decoded. Jinwen characters still looked like drawings, but on the whole their appearance was shapelier than those of Jiaguwen, with fuller and rounder strokes, much stronger linear features, and simpler forms. A significant difference was that Jinwen was first written with a brush and then inscribed onto the bronze ware, whereas Jiaguwen was carved with a knife. The brush effect of Jinwen created a sense of simplicity, vigour, and majesty. In the later period of the Western Zhou Dynasty, Jinwen reached its peak, with long inscriptions, regular arrangements, and aesthetic character forms.

The Appearance of Long Inscriptions. In the Shang Dynasty, inscriptions on bronze ware had very few characters, and some had as few as two. They were usually used to mark important vessels, and would give the name of the item, its owner, and why it was made. The largest bronze ding in ancient China was the Simuwu ding of the Shang Dynasty, weighing 875kg, which was unearthed from the ruins of Yin in Anyang, Henan Province. Inside it only three characters were inscribed, "Simuwu司母戊", which tell us that it was cast by Wu Ding, the emperor of the Shang Dynasty, when he held a sacrificial ceremony for his mother, "Wu." The longest inscription from the Shang Dynasty consisted of 42 characters. Inscriptions became longer in the Western Zhou Dynasty, with hundreds of characters appearing on each piece of bronze ware. They recorded events in great detail and carried messages of good fortune, such as "I wish you a long life" and "treasure your offspring forever." The longest inscription from the Western Zhou Dynasty, on the Maogong Ding, contained 497 characters, which together formed a long passage. The second longest had 357 characters, inscribed onto the underside of the Sanshi Plate of the Western Zhou Dynasty. The Maogong Ding, the Sanshi Plate and the Guojizi White Plate are collectively known as "the three great bronze ware pieces of the Western Zhou Dynasty." At the time of writing, the inscriptions on the bronze ware of the Western Zhou Dynasty are the longest known inscriptions from ancient China.

The Maogong Ding Tripod from the Western Zhou Dynasty
The Maogong Ding bears the longest inscription of all the bronze dings from Ancient China.

The Historical Value of Inscriptions.

To date, the inscriptions from the Shang and Zhou Dynasties have provided us with the most significant social and historical information on these eras. The above-mentioned Sanshi Plate, for example, used 357 characters to record a land dispute between two princely states under the control of the emperor of the Zhou Dynasty, and tells us a lot about the nature of ancient lawsuits. In 1976 a Ligui, a type of bronze item from the early Western Zhou Dynasty was unearthed. Its inscription of 32 characters revealed a great deal about the occasion of "herding a field battle," in which Emperor Wuwang of the Zhou Dynasty conquered Emperor Zhou of the Shang Dynasty. It clearly tells us that this vital battle was over within a day, and confirms the *Shi Ji* (*Record of History*) account that "On the day of Jiazi, the forces of the Shang Dynasty were defeated." The famous Dayu Ding bears an inscription of 291 characters, which tells the story of a nobleman called Yu from the Western Zhou Dynasty. He was commanded by Emperor Zhou of the dynasty not to idle his life away on leisure pursuits, and to instead devote his time and energy to serving his country. The 284 characters on the reverse of the Shiqiang Plate, a

Inscriptions on Ligui from the Western Zhou Dynasty

Shiqiang Plate from the Western Zhou
Dynasty

piece of Western Zhou bronze ware, praise the past emperors of the Zhou Dynasty and tell the family history of the Ding's creator. This tells us a great deal about the history of the Western Zhou Dynasty, and about the Zhou Dynasty's policies regarding the survivors of the Shang Dynasty, so ancient Chinese bronze ware has a very important historical value.

The Jinwen inscriptions on the bronze ware of the Shang and Zhou Dynasties were seen as items of wonder in the Bronze Age world. They formed a connection between the preceding Jiaguwen inscriptions and the later Xiaozhuan inscriptions (the lesser seal style adopted by the Qin Dynasty (221-206 BC)), and represented an equally important stage in the evolution of the Han characters. Jinwen characters looked like drawings, but they showed significant progress from the earlier pictographic and ideographic character forms, moving towards the square linear ideographic forms that we recognize today.

Muye Battle: "Zhou" was originally an old tribe, based on the Loess Plateau in western China and a state subject to the Shang Dynasty. In the later period of the dynasty, the ruling government had become very decadent, and Emperor Wuwang of the Zhou decided to crusade against the emperor of the Shang Dynasty. On the fifth day of the second lunar month (the day of Jiazi) in 1046 BC, Emperor Wu led 45,000 soldiers, 3,000 knights and 300 chariots, united with other tribes, to fight a decisive battle with the 100,000-strong army of the Emperor of the Shang Dynasty. As the battle progressed, the Shang's troops surrendered one-by-one and guided the Zhou's forces to conquer the Shang's capital, Chaoge. When the Shang emperor realized his kingdom was lost, he burned himself to death in a robe made of jade. The Shang Dynasty was defeated and the Western Zhou Dynasty was established. An inscription of 32 characters, found on Ligui, provides us with reliable material evidence of the specific time of the Muye Battle.

Ancient Artistic Characters: Xiaozhuan

Xiaozhuan (the lesser seal style of Chinese characters), was the result of the "writing in the same characters" policy, which was adopted by Emperor Qinshihuang of the Qin Dynasty (221-206 BC). This policy represented the first large-scale simplification and standardization of the Han characters, and resulted in their variant forms being rearranged. This took place during the Warring States Period (425-221 BC). The forms of the Xiaozhuan characters were simpler than those of their predecessors, and the composition of their lines was less like drawings. The emergence of Xiaozhuan marked the end of the ancient Chinese characters.

The variant forms of character "马 horse" and "安 peace" from the Warring States Period (475 - 221 BC)

The Emergence of Xiaozhuan. During the Warring States Period (475–221BC) Han characters were not standardized and had many variant forms. The 齐Qi, 楚Chu, 燕Yan, 韩Han, 赵Zhao, and 魏 Wei States in the East, and the 秦Qin State in the West, would employ different ways of writing each character, and in some cases, different ways of pronouncing them. After uniting China in 221 BC, Emperor Qinshihuang took immediate action to unify the characters, in order to resolve the inconsistencies in their use, and in turn strengthen his control over the country. He instigated the policy of "writing in the same characters," and ordered his Prime Minister, Li Si, to oversee the unification. He used the characters prevalent in the Qin State as the standard, and annulled the character forms found in the six Eastern States, retaining only those features he considered to be their finest, in order to establish a unified written language, known as Xiaozhuan.

Figure of Emperor Qinshihuang

Zhuan meant "drawing with crooked lines." Jiaguwen, Jinwen, and the characters of the Warring States Period (425-221 BC) were collectively known as Dazhuan

Emperor Qinshihuang: Emperor Qinshihuang, named Ying Zheng (259–210 BC), was the king of the Qin State in western China. He spent ten years conquering the six eastern states, ultimately uniting China in 221 BC, and subsequently established the first feudalist-centralized country in history. Emperor Qinshihuang was the first emperor of China. To safeguard the consolidation of his country, he adopted a policy of tyrannical domination. Meanwhile, he was responsible for many events of great historical importance. Besides unifying characters, scales of length, capacity and weight, and thought (burning books and burying Confucian scholars alive), he also built the Great Wall, laid roads, dug irrigation systems, fixed a universal size for carriages, and established counties (administrative regions), all of which greatly influenced later generations. It is difficult to express in words the significance of Emperor Qinshihuang's contribution to the historical and cultural development of China.

Xiaozhuan characters with beautiful forms

(large seal characters). The characters unified by Emperor Qinshihuang of the Qin Dynasty were called Xiaozhuan (meaning lesser seal characters) because they had a simpler structure than the Dazhuan ones. The development of Xiaozhuan in the Warring States Period represented the first large-scale simplification and standardization of the Han characters, and established a single, unified set.

Ancient Artistic Characters. The calligraphic characters of Xiaozhuan are considered the most beautiful in ancient China, and are known as the "artistic characters." Xiaozhuan's beauty lies in its ordered rectangular forms, its regular, symmetrical structure, its rounded and graceful strokes, and the even thickness of its lines. In comparison to Dazhuan, Xiaozhuan is simpler, and each character has only one written form. In terms of strokes, the right-angles of Dazhuan became more rounded in Xiaozhuan, and the number of strokes, and the forms and positions of the character components, also became fixed. In Xiaozhuan characters, the component that indicated meaning, for example, was usually written on the left-hand side of the character, and more components that indicated sound (pictophonetic characters), also appeared. On careful observation we can see occasional pictographic features in Xiaozhuan characters, but they are not obvious, which indicates that Xiaozhuan had largely moved away from drawings, and had become more abstract.

The Official Style of Characters in the Qin Dynasty. In the Qin Dynasty, Xiaozhuan was the official character style, and was used in all important government documents.

Bronze Tiger-shaped Tally from the Qin Dynasty, inscribed with Xiaozhuan characters

For example, when Emperor Qinshihuang standardized the measurements of length, capacity and weight, the inscriptions on the imperial bronze edicts that he issued across the country were written in Xiaozhuan. This is visible on many instruments of weight and measurement that have been unearthed from the Qin Dynasty, and also on excavated coins, eaves tiles, weapons, tiger-shaped lallies, and ancient steles from the era.

The Carved Stones of the Qin Dynasty

In 219 BC, after uniting China, Emperor Qinshihuang led a convoy of carts and horses to visit seven cities, and at each of them he set up a stone stele inscribed with his ideas. The inscriptions on the steles were written by Li Si in Xiaozhuan characters. Xiaozhuan characters had an ordered and precise structure, with rounded strokes, and a simple, vigorous style, and were known as "the orthodox school of Xiaozhuan." Of the seven steles, only the Taishan Carved Stone and the Langyatai Carved Stone still exist today, and most of their original stone inscriptions have been destroyed. Five other carved stones exist, including the Yishan Carved stone, but these are later imitations of the originals.

Xiaozhuan Characters inscribed onto bronze coins from the Han Dynasty

The two characters of "半两 semi-tael" in Xiaozhuan Style on currency. According to legend these were personally written by Li Si.

Rubbings of the Taishan Carving Stone by Emperor Qinshihuang
These Xiaozhuan style characters inscribed onto stone are believed to have been personally written by Li Si. A few of them have been preserved to the present day, giving this stone great historical value. It is now kept in Tai'an Dai Temple in Shandong Province.

Rubbings of the inscriptions on bronze imperial edicts, from the Qin Dynasty

Rubbings of the Yishan Carved Stone by Emperor Qinshihuang
The Xiaozhuan characters on these carved stones have regular and symmetric forms, and rounded and visually pleasing strokes. They demonstrate the beauty of curved-line calligraphy.

Modern Characters Dissimilar to Drawings

In the Qin Dynasty, when scholars of a lower stature wrote Xiaozhuan (the lesser seal style) characters on bamboo and wood, little did they know that they were creating a whole new style of calligraphy. This new style was called Lishu, the official script. The emergence of Lishu represented a major landmark in the development of the Han characters, as it no longer contained pictographic characters, and so a new phase in their history was entered.

Bamboo Strips of Lishu of the Han Dynasty Unearthed from Wuwei, Gansu Province

Great Changes in the Forms of the Han Characters

After Xiaozhuan, the Han characters entered the phase of the "modern characters," and the calligraphic styles in which they were written included Lishu (the official script) and Kasha (the regular script). Lishu saw the forms of the Han characters break away from drawings, as they came to be composed of strokes and symbols that were no longer pictographic, but indicative. This evolution from pictographic to indicative symbols marked a great change in the Han script, and was a stage of great significance in the history of Chinese characters.

The Demarcation Line between Ancient and Modern Characters: Lishu

In the Qin Dynasty, while Xiaozhuan remained popular, a faster and more convenient style had become popular with the ordinary people. This style was known as Lishu, which developed in full during the Han Dynasty (206 BC-220 AD). The structures of the Lishu characters were composed of straight strokes and simplified forms. They were completely different from drawings, having transformed into pure symbols, and after that point the Han characters were standardized. Lishu broke the pictographic mould of the ancient characters, ending their era and paving the way for the modern characters we see today.

Wood-Bark Volumes from the Han Dynasty, found in Juyan

The Contribution of Yamen Servants. Paper was invented during the Western Han Dynasty (206 BC – 25 AD), but it was not widely adopted until the end of the Eastern Han Dynasty (25-220). In the Qin Dynasty and the Warring States Period people would usually paint characters onto strips of bamboo or wood, using brushes. In order to write more quickly, the Yamen servants, whose job was to compose official documents, adopted the calligraphic style most popular with the ordinary people, turning the rounded strokes of Xiaozhuan (the lesser seal style) into straight lines, and simplifying their form, enabling them to be written more quickly. This new style of simplified

Juyan Bamboo and Wood Strips from the Han Dynasty: The watershed of the Ejinahe River in present day Inner Mongolia, northwest China, was the region of "Juyan" in the Han Dynasty. There the government of the Western Han Dynasty stationed armies, developed wasteland, and established towns. Juyan also became a station on the ancient "Silk Road," and so came to be known as "Juyan Way." Since 1930 archaeologists have conducted three great excavations of the area, unearthing more than 30,000 examples of bamboo and wood strips from the Han Dynasty. It is this site from which the most bamboo and wood strips have been excavated in China, the majority of them being wood, and relatively few being bamboo. They record various aspects of the Han Dynasty, such as politics, military affairs, economy, and daily life, and have a very high historical value. Meanwhile the lively Lishu characters found on strips of bark reflect the style of folk calligraphy in the Han Dynasty.

Ruins of Heicheng Town in Juyan
Since the 1930s, strips of bamboo and wood from the Han Dynasty have continuously been excavated from here.

Change to Lishu: The evolution of the Han characters from Xiaozhuan to Lishu is known as "the change to Lishu." It was a major event in the characters' historical development and a represented a great revolution in written Chinese language. It was not only the most important stage of simplification in the evolution of the Han characters; it also marked the end of the "ancient characters" phase, and the beginning of that of the "modern characters." After the change to Lishu, the Han characters' lines changed from bent to straight, their pictographic features disappeared, and they began to take on a new style that was composed completely of strokes. In short, the previously drawing-like "line characters" became "stroke characters." From that point on, the characters no longer resembled drawings; they were simpler and more symbolic, and as a result, much easier to learn and write.

calligraphy was called Lishu because it was created by officials with lower positions, known as the Li people. We can be quite certain that Lishu was created from the drawing of Xiaozhuan characters with brush pens and accelerated writing. Many examples of Lishu can be found on excavated bamboo and wooden strips, such as those from the Qin State of Shuihudi, Yunmeng. The forms of the Lishu characters on those strips were completely different from Xiaozhuan. More than 30,000 pieces of the famous Juyan Han strips have been discovered, and the Lishu characters painted onto them show both the artistic quality of calligraphy during the Han Dynasty, and the liberal and relaxed approach of its writers. According to archaeological evidence, Lishu became a popular calligraphic style in the Qin Dynasty, alongside Xiaozhuan. In the Han Dynasty Lishu had come into common use across the board, by everyone from government officials down to ordinary people.

The Change to Lishu: The Great Revolution of the Characters.

Lishu represented a great simplification in the forms of the Xiaozhuan characters. Its structure, composed of strokes and indicative symbols, made the pictographic nature of the Xiaozhuan characters obsolete, as the Han characters became ideographic. As a result of Lishu, the modern Han characters came

Dazhuan
(Large Seal Characters)

Xiaozhuan
(Lesser Seal Characters)

Lishu
(Official Script)

Dazhuan
(Big Seal Characters)

Xiaozhuan
(Lesser Seal Characters)

Lishu
(Official Script)

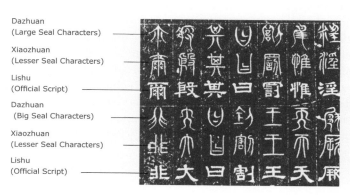

Rubbings of the *Santi Shijing* from the Three Kingdoms (220 – 280 AD) In comparison to Dazhuan and Xiaozhuan, the forms of Lishu characters have clearly moved away from drawings.

	烏	燕	魚	馬
Xiaozhuan(Lesser Seal Characters)	𩾏	燕	魚	馬
Lishu (Official Script)	烏	燕	魚	馬

Many different strokes from Xiaozhuan were reproduced in Lishu.

to bear no resemblance to drawings. We can conclude that Lishu represented the demarcation line between the ancient and modern characters; that is, before Lishu, characters had taken the form of "ancient characters," being closer to drawings, and with the arrival of Lishu, they took the form of "modern characters" which made a departure from drawings. The evolution from Xhuanshu to Lishu in the Han characters is known as "the change to Lishu," which is seen as a very significant revolution.

The Features of Han Li. Han Li is the Lishu script of the Han Dynasty. The forms of the Han Li characters had progressed from square to oblate forms, the older drawing-like lines had totally disappeared, and the strokes were no longer rounded, with wave shapes exhibiting changes in thickness and force. In Han Li, a horizontal stroke has three turns with a wave, the endings of the horizontal, left-falling and right-falling strokes rise upwards, and the left-falling and right-falling strokes extend on both sides. The strokes of Han Li are extended forcefully with symmetrical forms, and its wave-like shapes are its most distinctive feature. The components of the Xiaozhuan characters also became simplified in Lishu; for example the components of "水water", "手hand" and "心heart" in Xiaozhuan became "氵", "扌", and "忄" as the left components of Lishu characters. Many of the main components of Xiaozhuan were also simplified; for example the claw and tail in the Xiaozhuan character "鸟bird", the tails in the two characters "燕swallow", and "鱼fish", and the leg and tail in the character "马horse", all became just four dots in the Han Li characters. The simplified forms of the Lishu style made the Han characters easier to write.

The Elegant Style of Han Li. Many Lishu characters have been preserved on strips of bamboo and wood, and on stone steles, and the highest achievements of ancient Lishu are displayed on the stele inscriptions of the Eastern Han Dynasty. A large number of Lishu stele inscriptions exist from the dynasty, which vary stylistically and are highly sophisticated. Examples are the Stele of Sacrificial Vessels, with its solemn but attractive calligraphic style, the elegant Yiying Stele, the sturdy and simple Zhangqian Stele, the unrestrained Ode to Shimen in its various forms, and the lively *Ode to Xixia*, all of which are regarded as excellent models for students of calligraphy to follow. In 175 Cai Yong, a great scholar of the Eastern Han Dynasty, collaborated with others to write some major Confucian classics in the Lishu style, such as *Shi Jing* (*Classics of Poetry*), *Shang Shu*, and *The Analects of Confucius*. Famous craftsmen then carved them onto 46 stone steles, which were set up at the door of Luoyang Taixue (the Imperial College), and were known as the famous *Xiping Shijing*. Many intellectuals are said to have come to Luoyang to see and learn *Shijing*, arriving in over 1,000 carriages that blocked the road. The *Xiping Shijing* is the earliest official Confucian classic in China. The Lishu characters inscribed on it have become the standard representative works of Han Li, and are regarded as masterpieces. Only a few relics of the *Xiping Shijing* have survived to the present day.

The beautiful and elegant *Yiying Stele* of the Eastern Han Dynasty (25 – 220 AD)

The calm, unhurried and graceful *Shichen Stele* of the Eastern Han Dynasty (25 – 220 AD)

The lively and vigorous *Ode to Xixia* from the Eastern Han Dynasty (25-220)

Kaishu: The Standard Style of Calligraphy

Kaishu (regular script), also known as "Zenshu" (meaning real script) or "Zengshu" (meaning regular script), was given its name because it was used as a model for learning calligraphy. Kaishu emerged at the end of the Eastern Han Dynasty and evolved from Lishu (Han Li). During the Sui (581-618) and Tang (618-907) dynasties, it advanced considerably. Kaishu is easier to write than Lishu and easier to read than Caoshu (a cursive hand), so it is still popular even today, and has become the standard style of calligraphy, with the most diverse and longest running usage.

Upright and Square Han Characters. It is said that in the Three Kingdoms (220-280), Shong You, a minister of the Wei State, wrote the earliest Kaishu characters. He turned the wave-like strokes of Lishu into horizontal and vertical lines, and stopped making the endings of the horizontal, left-falling and right-falling strokes rise upwards. He also introduced the hook stroke, and the characters' forms became upright and square. These changes represented a simplification, and made the characters easier to write. Kaishu characters have square forms, precise and symmetrical structures, and generous and aesthetic strokes, and are completely closed. Kaishu and Lishu have the same basic structure and form, and differ only in terms of their strokes. The strokes of Kaishu are straight, and unlike Lishu, they have no waves, and do not rise at the ends.

Lishu (Official Script)	春江花月夜
Kaishu (Regular Script)	春江花月夜

Comparison between Lishu and Kaishu Strokes
The strokes of Kaishu have clearly lost the waves that characterised Lishu, and the ends of some of its strokes no longer rise upwards.

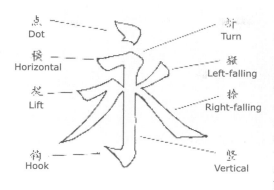

Dot

Horizontal

Lift

Hook

Turn

Left-falling

Right-falling

Vertical

Illustration of Eight Strokes in the Character "永Yong"

The Eight Strokes of the Character "Yong". In ancient times the eight strokes of the character "永", used for learning Kaishu, clearly demonstrated the eight basic strokes of the style: dot, horizontal, vertical, left-falling, right-falling, turn, lift, and hook stroke. Repeatedly writing the character "永" was an effective way of learning the basic strokes of Kaishu, and was widely adopted by the ancient people.

Yan Zhenqing (709 - 785)

Yan Tendon and Liu Bone. Ancient calligraphers who practiced Kaishu exhibited different stroke styles. For example Yan Zhenqing of the Tang Dynasty (618-907) produced full and sturdy strokes, whereas Liu Gongquan created thin and rigid ones. Because of this, the phrase "Yan tendon and Liu bone," or "Yan fat and Liu thin" was coined to describe their different styles. Other examples are the Kaishu characters of Ouyang Xun from the Tang Dynasty, which were round, fluent, square and forceful, and those of Zhao Mengfu in the Yuan Dynasty (1206-1368), which were also round and fluent. People still refer to Yan Zhenqing, Liu Gongquan, Ouyang Xun and Zhao Mengfu as the four great ancient Kaishu calligraphers.

The Most Common Character Styles. The Han characters printed and handwritten today are in the Kaishu style. Since the invention of printing in the Song Dynasty (960-1279), Kaishu has been the mainstream style used in books, magazines and newspapers. Kaishu has several variants for these purposes: Songti or Song-Dynasty style, Fangsongti (an imitation of the Song-Dynasty style), and Heiti (boldface style). These print-style characters

Kaishu by Yan Zhenqing   Kaishu by Liu Gongquan   Kaishu by Ouyang Xun   Kaishu by Zhao Mengfu

are graded according to size, and adapted to suit different types of printing. Print-style characters have horizontal or vertical strokes, are clear, ordered and symmetrical, and are generally favoured by the reading public. They represent a simplification of the Kaishu forms, which has made them easier to use.

Kaishu represents the final stage in the evolution of Chinese characters. Since the formation of Kaishu there have been very few further changes, except for some minor structural simplifications.

A Lively and Vigorous Cursive Hand

The cursive hand refers to the writing of Lishu characters in a simplified and continuous way. It breaks the square forms of the Han characters, with "fluttering" lines and connected strokes, giving it a lively and vigorous appearance. As it is hard to read characters written in this way, the cursive hand is not a very practical style, but it is aesthetically pleasing. The cursive hand is divided into Zhangcao, Jincao and Kuangcao. The written Kuangcao characters are widely admired as works of art. China can boast many masters of cursive-hand calligraphy, such as Zhang Xu, a great calligrapher of the Tang Dynasty (618-907). His Kuangcao works are free, bold, unrestrained, and

Gushi Sitie (Four Old Poems) by Zhang Xu (Part) in highly cursive hand

full of motion and enthusiasm. People highly respect his cursive-hand works, and regard him as "the master of cursive handwriting."

The Fluent and Practical Running Hand

Wang Xizhi, a Master of Calligraphy

Running hand is the result of Lishu being written rapidly, meaning that the characters are neither as ordered as Kaishu, nor as elegant as cursive writing. As a style it sits somewhere between regular script and cursive hand, and is easy to recognize. If we liken Kaishu to "sitting," and cursive hand to "flying," we could describe running hand as "walking." Running hand is extremely practical, and is typically used in everyday writing. In ancient China there were many great calligraphers of running hand, such as Wang Xizhi of the Eastern Jin Dynasty (317-420). He was hailed "the master of calligraphy," and his outstanding talent was demonstrated in Kaishu, running hand and cursive hand. The *Lang Ting Xu*, written by Wang Xizhi in running hand style, displays beautifully formed characters and fluent strokes, earning it the title of "the number one running hand work in the world."

Lan Ting Xu by Wang Xizhi (detail, imitation copy of the Tang Dynasty), in running hand

The Development of Mainstream Han Characters

Well-formed characters have clear meanings and can be written quickly. In the course of their development, the Han characters have continued to be simplified. While their forms are in some ways complex, so that their meaning can be accurately conveyed, simplification has always been key to their development. The history of Han characters is a history of continuous simplification.

If a character has two forms, the one with the most strokes is called a complex character, whereas the one with the least strokes is called a simplified character. Complex and simplified characters have co-existed since ancient times, as the process of simplification has continued.

The Simplification of the Han Characters through History

For hundreds, even thousands of years, Han characters have posed a problem: they are difficult to learn, write, and memorise.

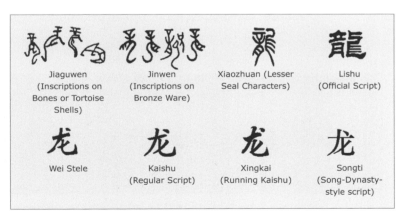

| Jiaguwen (Inscriptions on Bones or Tortoise Shells) | Jinwen (Inscriptions on Bronze Ware) | Xiaozhuan (Lesser Seal Characters) | Lishu (Official Script) |
| Wei Stele | Kaishu (Regular Script) | Xingkai (Running Kaishu) | Songti (Song-Dynasty-style script) |

Illustration Based on the Evolution of the Han Characters' Forms

Flourishing Scene of Ancient Suzhou
In ancient times, the ordinary people continuously created simplified characters using simple strokes. These were known as "common-form characters."

Simplification of the Character "车 (车)che"
The pictographic characters in this picture are all ancient versions of "车". They provide a vivid illustration of ancient chariots. The main picture is the wood chariot (a reproduction) from the Shang Dynasty; excavated from Anyang, Henan Province.

In order to resolve this, people have continuously tried to simplify them, a process that has shaped their history. Since ancient times the characters have undergone several simplifications, such as the evolution from Dazhuan to Xiaozhuan, and from Zhuanshu to Lishu. Ordinary people have since simplified them further by using less complex strokes. Most of the current simplified characters are called "standard forms." Some people believe that ancient philologists first created these in their studies, but this is not true.

Ancient Simplified Characters
These common-form characters, created and used by ancient people, have become standard simplified characters that are in everyday use today.

云	网	胡	电	从	众	虫	来	杯
寿	与	发	声	怜	亲	旧	当	党
亚	坏	凤	总	灯	战	机	虽	担
务	边	实	尔	无	气	礼	个	处
宝	时	节	声	梦	厅	灵	远	劝

The Simplification of the Han Characters Today

Since the foundation of the People's Republic of China in 1949, the Chinese Government has simplified the Han characters as part of a major programme of standardization. This principally covers two aspects: a reduction in strokes and a reduction in the number of characters. The current simplified characters used in mainland China are the result of an ongoing study conducted by the Chinese Government since 1956. In 1964 it issued the General Table of Simplified Characters, following it with a further updated version in 1986. A total of 2,263 complex characters have been replaced by 2,235 simplified characters, representing one-third of the total current characters. After simplification, the Han characters' strokes were reduced by nearly 50 percent, and as a result, the speed at which they could be written increased.

Reduction of Strokes. The simplification of the characters principally involved a reduction in the number of strokes they contained. For example, "貝 bei" was simplified to "贝", and "優 you" was simplified to "优". "贝" and "优", with fewer strokes are also simplified characters. Many simplified characters can serve as components, so a large group of Han characters have fewer strokes, such as "财 cai", "购 gou", "资 zi", and "贵 gui", with "贝" as a component. The simplified characters have more concise forms than the complex ones, and have become popular because they are easier to learn and quicker to write.

Simplify Components	貓→猫	億→亿	蘋→苹
Preserve Outline	龜→龟	來→来	齒→齿
Replace with Homophones	穀→谷	後→后	幾→几
Replace with Symbols	漢→汉	艱→艰	歡→欢
Create Kaishu Forms of Cursive–hand Characters	書→书	長→长	學→学
Use Parts	飛→飞	聲→声	開→开
Adopt Ancient Forms	塵→尘	雲→云	從→从

Major Methods for Simplifying the Han Characters

杯──盃	略──畧	启──啟
哲──喆	岳──嶽	峰──峯
考──攷	群──羣	同──仝
叫──呌	采──採	布──佈
决──決	辉──煇	减──減
迹──蹟、跡	回──囬、囘、廻	

Examples of Common Variant Forms
In each group, the former is the standard character and the latter is the discontinued variant form.

The reduction in the characters' strokes has meant that they have lost their cultural connotations; however their main function is for writing, rather than cultural expression.

Today, any characters that do not comply with the General Table of Simplified Characters are not considered to be standard characters, such as the complex characters "學(学)xue" and "習(习) xi", which now have simplified forms. Simplified characters that are not included in the General Table, or that have been created by individuals, such as "(街)", "(道)", "(场)", "(展)" and "(餐)", are not supposed be used. It should be noted here that although complex characters are not standard characters, they are not incorrect. They still appear in books, in the study of Chinese, and in works of calligraphy.

In recent times, simplified characters have become more and more widely used. Both the Chinese mainland and the international community have adopted them. Chinese versions of UN documents use simplified characters, and more than 1.3 billion people currently use them on a daily basis.

Reduction in the Number of Characters. The second way in which the Han characters have been simplified, is a reduction in their number. This has mainly involved abolishing "variant forms" - characters that have the same pronunciation and meaning, but are written in different ways. The abolishment of variant forms involves preserving one way of writing a character in favour of all others. For example the character "决jue" in the phrase "解决jiejue" (solve), cannot be written as "決". The latter is a variant form, and so can no longer be used.

Simplified characters are convenient to write, and also demonstrate their creators' wisdom. Ancient China witnessed many great processes of simplification, and the simplified characters we see in mainland China today represent another of these. It is hoped that simplified characters will continue to benefit ordinary people for years to come, and their simplification is expected to continue into the future.

Among the current Han characters, there are some that still have many strokes and complex structures, such as 餐(can), 警(jing), 鼻(bi), 籍(ji), 嚼(jiao), 藏(cang), 舞(wu), 繁(fan), 微(wei), 赢(ying), 嘴(zui), 鹰(ying), 翻(fan), 鼠(shu), 爆(bao), and 懂(dong). These characters are all in common use and need to be simplified, as they are still very difficult to learn and write.

The Han characters have been through three distinct stages of development, namely primitive drawing-like characters, ancient characters, and modern characters, a process that has taken at least 5,000 years. In terms of the evolution of their form, from Jiaguwen (inscriptions on animal bones and tortoiseshells) to the modern Han characters, they have progressed from drawings to strokes, from pictographic to symbolic characters, and from complex to simple characters. The progression from drawing-like "line characters" to "stroke characters," and their consequent simplification, has been central to the characters' development.

The Formation of the Han Characters

Han characters originated from drawings, and the earliest characters appeared in the form of paintings of things people saw. The total number of Han characters is between 50,000 and 60,000. It would be impossible to create this many characters solely from drawings, so from very early on, the ancient Chinese people formed Han characters using four methods: pictograph, indication, associative compounds, and phonograms.

The Ancient Formation of the "Six Categories"

The *Shuowen Jiezi* (*Origin of Chinese Characters*), was a famous study of the Han characters written during the Eastern Han Dynasty (25 – 220). In it the author, Xu Shen, organized the ancient Han characters into "six categories." These categories made distinctions between form, pronunciation and meaning, and showed how they were integrated, breaking new ground in the study of ancient Chinese characters. The *Shuowen Jiezi* preserves a wealth of information on ancient characters, making it a lasting and invaluable resource for students and scholars of Chinese philology.

Xu Shen

Xu Shen, who lived during the Eastern Han Dynasty (25-220) was a famous philologist in ancient China. He studied the formation of Han characters and wrote the famous *Shouwen Jiezi* (*Origin of Chinese Characters*), in which he examined the characters' structure using his "six category" theory. He was the first person to make a full analysis of each of their components, and the *Shuowen Jiezi* served as the first dictionary of ancient Chinese.

Figure of Xu Shen

The Contention between Ancient-Character and Modern-Character Studies of the Confucian Classics

In the Western Han Dynasty (206 BC – 25 AD), Emperor Han Wudi (157 – 87 BC) adopted the ideas of Confucius and Mengzi, such as the feudalist domination philosophy, in order to unify

Dacheng Hall, the house of Confucius
It is believed that when Emperor Qinshihuang of the Qin Dynasty burnt Confucian books, Confucius surviving relatives hid many of his classics, written in Dazhuan characters, inside the walls of Confucius' house. These included the *Analects of Confucius*, *Shang Shu*, and *Chun Qiu* (*The Spring and Autumn Annals*). They were discovered during the reign of Emperor Wudi of the Western Han Dynasty (206 BC - 25 AD). These Confucian texts written in Dazhuan characters are examples of ancient-character classics.

his state. As a result, the Confucian classics became a popular subject of study. Emperor Han Wudi set up "Taixue," the Imperial College of the Capital in Ancient Times, in the city of Chang'an (the present-day Xi'an), where they could be studied. He also employed the prestigious "five classics court academics," the equivalent to modern-day professors, to teach them. At the time, the classics were written in the popular Lishu style, which belonged to the school of "modern characters," and so became known as the "modern character classics." At the end of Emperor Han Wudi's reign, some classics written in Dazhuan, which were "ancient characters," were found inside the walls of Confucius' old house, and they have become known as the "ancient character classics." The appearance of Confucius' works in two different types of character resulted in some contention over their meaning, and the consequent disagreement between the schools of ancient and modern character classics went on for at least 200 years. Xu Shen, who himself belonged to the ancient character classics school, spent 22 years writing the *Shouwen*

Jiezi (*Origin of Chinese Characters*), and his careful analysis of the characters' structure helps us to explain the ancient and modern character classics more accurately.

The *Shuowen Jiezi* (*Origin of Chinese Characters*)

The *Shuowen Jiezi* consists of 15 volumes, in which 9,353 characters are listed and organized into 540 components. Focusing mainly on Xiaozhuan, Xu Shen analysed the structures of written Chinese, and comprehensively explained their form, pronunciation and meaning. By associating the Xiaozhuan characters' meanings with their forms, he enabled readers to learn both their structures and their original meanings. The book became the first dictionary of ancient Chinese, and still serves as today a useful reference work on ancient writing. Xu Shen did not see any Jiaguwen characters, meaning that not all of his analyses are reliable, but on the whole they are considered correct. Xu Shen's method of integrating form, pronunciation and meaning, and then indexing the characters based

A copy of the first page in the component category of "丝Si" in the *Shuowen Jiezi* (*Origin of Chinese Characters*)

All the characters in the category of "丝si" have the component "纟", and the first listed "糸" Xiaozhuan style is the component.

Components: The system of components was established for ease of dictionary reference, and invented by Xu Shen. In his *Shuowen Jiezi* (*Origin of Chinese Characters*), he classified 9,353 characters into 540 categories. All the characters within a category had the same component, and the first character in each category was its component. Therefore there were 540 components, each component representing a major "category." In the *Shuowen Jiezi*, 540 components represented 540 categories, and each category included many things. Nowadays a dictionary usually has more than 200 components, covering tens of thousands of Han characters. The establishment of a component system not only makes characters easier to look up in a dictionary, but also gives prominence to their meanings. This is extremely useful for learning and using them. Regarding the current major dictionaries of Chinese, there are presently 214 components in *Ci Yuan* (*Origin of Vocabularies*), 200 in *Hanyu Dazidian* and *Hanyu Dacidian* (*Grand Chinese Dictionary*), 250 in *Ci Hai* (*The Sea of Vocabulary*), 189 in *Xinhua Zidian* (*Xinhua Dictionary*), and 201 in *Xiandai Hanyu Changyong Zibiao* (*Table of Common Characters in Modern Chinese Language*).

on their components, provided a wealth of information on ancient Chinese writing. It has been preserved as an important resource in the study of Han philology.

In the *Shuowen Jiezi*, Xu Shen proposed "six categories" of Han characters, namely pictographic characters, indicative characters, associative compounds, phonograms, mutually explanatory characters, and phonetic loan characters. By integrating these six categories, he was able to analyse the formation of 9,353 Han characters. Late philologists believed, however, that two of Xu Shen's categories – mutually explanatory and phonetic loan characters – actually relate to how they were used, rather than how they were created. Xu Shen's "six character" analysis of the ancient characters remains one of the most significant contributions to the philology of Chinese writing, and still plays a major role in the analysis of modern Han characters. Almost 50 percent of the current simplified characters we read and use today, can be analysed in terms of the "six categories" principle.

Methods of Forming the Han Characters

After the Han characters appeared, they were categorized in terms of the different methods used in forming them. Learning how to form Han characters involves learning their structure. The methods for forming the characters are more important than how the forms evolved, because while the latter is concerned only with the physical act of writing, the former determines the essential changes that the characters have undergone. In the *Shuowen Jiezi* the "six categories" principle is used to explain the six methods involved in forming characters for everyday language. There are, in fact, only four formation methods: pictograph, indication, associative compounds, and indications of meaning and sound – the first four of the six categories. The characters formed using those four methods are referred to respectively as pictographic, indicative, associative-compound, and pictophonetic. The first three are purely graphic characters, whose meaning lies in their form, and no pronunciation is indicated. Pictophonetic characters, on the other hand, are semi-graphic and semi-phonetic. While mutually explanatory characters are less important in the history of the Han characters, phonetic loan characters played an important role in their development. Philologists believe that a combination of mutually explanatory and phonetic loan characters resulted in the characters taking on a wider range of uses, just like the formation of the characters themselves.

Drawing the Shapes of Things: Pictographic Characters

Readable "Drawings." Ancient Chinese people used themselves, along with animals and all of the natural things around them, as models for drawing, and thereby created drawing-like pictographic characters. The first characters that were created all represented nouns, and indicated both meaning and pronunciation. For example, "日" looks like the sun and is pronounced rì, "山" looks like mountain peaks and is pronounced shān, "人" looks like

Jiaguwen
The pictographic characters in the famous cattle-bone inscriptions from the Shang Dynasty are very vivid.

the profile of a person and is pronounced rén, and "鹿" looks like a small running deer and is articulated as lù. They all have pronunciation, making them characters rather than simply drawings.

Drawing the Features of Objects. The ancient pictographic characters can be likened to drawings because they show the typical features of the things they represent. For example, the round "日, sun", bent "月, moon", stable "山, mountain", flowing "水, water", standing "人, person", big-headed "子, boy", posture of "女, girl", horns of "鹿, deer", mane of "马,

Pictographic characters were created on the basis of everyday human experience and had distinctive features.

The ancient people illustrated natural things in the form of pictographic characters.

The pictographic characters that represented animals depicted their typical features.

Some of the new, simplified pictographic characters have more distinguishing pictographic features than the complex characters.

CHINESE CHARACTERS

Writer's Pen Painting, in Pictographic Han Characters
This painting shows the pictographic and artistic qualities of some of the ancient Han characters, such as 日ri (sun), 月yue (moon), 明ming (bright), 女nu (girl), 目mu (eye), 泪 lei (tear), 木mu (tree), 鸟niao (bird), 集ji (perch), 牛niu (ox), 羊yang (sheep), 牢lao (pen), 犬 quan (dog), 京jing (artificial mound), 火huo (fire), 止zhi (foot), 手shou (hand) and 草cao (grass).

Guernica, by Picasso
Picasso used distorted forms and symbolic methods to compose this scene expressing human misery. It reveals the atrocities committed by German fascists when their air force bombed the small Spanish town of Guernica, and shows great artistic inspiration.

horse", straight horns of "牛, ox", curved horns of "羊, sheep", long trunk of "象, elephant", rolled-up tail of "犬, dog", fat body and downward-pointing tail of "猪, pig", and teeth and long, thin tail of "鼠, mouse", were all painted precisely and vividly. They look like exquisite works of art, with a lively style and a strong abstract quality.

Abstract Line Art. With their bases in ancient pictographic characters, the pictographic Han characters differ from those of other languages. They have concise lines, and are simultaneously real and not real, being abstract while also representing the typical features of objects. The ancient pictographic characters are all vivid and lively, and their abstract and artistic qualities have been likened to the works of Picasso, the great Spanish painter.

Pictographic Interest. The forms of the Ancient Han characters are very interesting pictographically, and even today's Kaishu characters, while no longer being pictographic, also look a bit like paintings. For example, the Kaishu character "xiao (smile)" looks just like a real smile, and is believed to make the reader happy. The character "xi (happy)" also bears a resemblance to an open-mouthed smile and is believed to express joy. The character "ku (cry)" looks like a person crying, and is said to make the reader feel sad. The character "shuai (cast)", which we see at the entrances to shops, indicating "on sale", looks like a hand throwing things out onto the street, and represents a shopkeeper throwing money away. In the marketplace, the character "串 chuan (kebab)" resembles a large mutton kebab, and is used to attract customers. Even people who do not know Chinese characters can understand "凸 tu (protruding)" and "凹 ao (concave)". The character "勺 sháo (spoon)" shows a handle and food, and is intended to make the reader smile. Some phrases also use the forms of the characters to describe the features of objects, such as 国字脸 (a face with a form like the character "国"), 八字胡 (a moustache with a form like character "八"), 八字腿 (which graphically represents a pair of legs by means of "八"), and 丁字尺 (a ruler formed like the character "丁"). These are all interesting examples in the study of Chinese characters.

Pictographic characters would ideally represent the forms of all things, but this is impossible because there are so many abstract concepts in language. Therefore there are relatively few pictographic characters in Chinese; only around 300 out of a total of 9,353 listed in the *Shuowen Jiezi*. However pictographic characters are still the basis of the Han characters' formation.

笑 xiao (smile), and 哭 ku (cry)

Adding Signs to Drawings: Indicative Characters

Indicative characters use symbolic signs, or add indicative signs to pictographic characters, in order to convey meaning. They are also known as "independent characters." Numeric characters, such as "一 yi (one)", "二 er (two)", and "三 san (three)", are typical indicative characters containing symbolic signs. "本 ben (root)", "刃 ren (blade)", and "甘 gan (sweet)", are all indicative characters with indicative signs added to the pictographic forms. For example, the dot added at the edge of the pictographic character "刀 dao (knife)", indicates the blade "刃" of a knife. The cross line added at the bottom of the pictographic character "木 mu (tree)" represents the root "X" of the tree. The cross line inserted inside the pictographic character "口 kou (mouth)" indicates something with a sweet taste, because "甘 gan (sweet)" means sweet. Other characters such as "上 shang (up)", "下 xia (down)", "末 mo (end)", "亦 yi (also)", and

Formation of the indicative characters "本 ben (root)", "刃 ren (blade)", and "甘 gan (sweet)".

"血xue (blood)" are all common indicative characters, which contain indicative signs. While indicative characters can express simple abstract concepts, they cannot easily express complex concepts, so there are very few indicative Han characters; only about 100 are listed in the *Shuowen Jiezi*.

Combined Drawings: Associative-Compound Characters

In ancient times, large totems were composed of several small ones – for example, the Chinese dragon. Associative-compound characters were also formed in this way. Two or more pictographic characters – "drawings" – were combined to form new characters and express new meanings. Both the forms and meanings of the new characters, then, were compounds. The formation of associative-compound characters is flexible, and represents more than just the sum of pictographic and indicative characters. Associative-compound characters have a carefully crafted structure and are the most interesting of all the characters. They fall into two categories: those with compounds of the same forms, and those with compounds of different forms.

Let's take a look at the associative-compound character "爨 cuàn (cook)". This character "爨" means "cook," and is composed of several pictographic characters with many strokes. In terms of its Xiaozhuan character form, the upper part is a "甑 zeng (vessel for steaming food)" showing the double handles of a kitchen oven, and the lower part represents two hands putting burning logs into it. The whole character illustrates the action of cooking. A person who does not know this character, can still understand from looking at it that it means "fire" and "cooking." This character is rarely used today and has no simplified form. It is said to be the most complex and interesting associative-compound character.

Associative-compound characters are divided into two categories: same- and different-compound characters.

Formation of the Associative-Compound Character "爨cuàn (cook)". The character "爨cuàn (cook)" is actually a drawing that illustrates the act of cooking in ancient times. On the left is the Xiaozhuan character of "爨cuàn (cook)" which on careful observation is extremely pictographic.

Combined Totems in Ancient Times
Large totems, composed of two or more objects (or totems), shed light on the formation of associative-compound characters, and indeed, some of them have been analyzed as associative-compound characters. This picture shows three famous large combined totems belonging to ancient clans: the Banpo totem of a fish with a human face, from Yangshao Culture (left), the totem of a holy man with the face of an animal, from Liangzhu Culture (center), and a totem of the character "旦dan (dawn)", from the Dawenkou Culture (right).

Two types of Associative-Compound Character: Same- and Different-Compound Characters

Same-Compound Characters. Each same-compound character is composed of several identical characters. For example, "(林) lin (woods)" is composed of two "木mu (tree)" and represents a wood that consists of more than one tree. "(森) sen (forest)" is composed of three "木mu (tree)", and represents a forest that consists of multiple trees. The meanings of "林" and "森" are formed from compounds of two or three repeated characters, and so are known as same-compound characters. Other common same-compound characters include "北bei (north)", "从cong (follow)", "炎yan (very hot)", "磊lei (heap of stones)", "淼miao (expanse of water)", and "晶jing (brilliant)".

Different-Compound Characters. Each different-compound character is composed of several different characters. For example, "休xiu (have a rest)" is composed of two different characters, i.e. "人ren (a person)" and "木mu (tree)." A person relaxing against a tree means "taking a rest." "明 ming (bright)" is composed of two characters that depict "shining", i.e. "日ri (sun)" and "月yue (moon)", and means "an abundance of light." The meanings of the two characters combine to form the meaning of the compound character – in this case, two different-compound

北 (🦵) (bei): Two people standing back-to-back, indicating opposition.

从 (🦵) (cong): Two people facing left, one behind the other, indicating the act of following.

比 (🦵) (bi): Two people facing right, one behind the other, indicating comparison.

化 (🦵) (hua): Two people upside down, indicating change.

众 (🦵) (zhong): This shows three people, indicating multitude.

Same-compound characters, composed of the character "人 ren (person)".

characters. Other common different-compound characters include "安 an (safe)", "友 you (friend)", "看 kan (look)", "见 jian (see)", "宿 su (lodge for the night)", and "寒 han (cold)". In Han script there are a comparatively high number of associative compound characters, which express meaning through combination.

Some interesting different-compound characters:

见 (🦵) (jian, see)

This character is composed of "目 mu (eye)", and "人 ren (person)". It depicted a very large eye in order to indicate the act of seeing something, i.e. something "shining before one's eye". "见 jian (see)" is different from "看 kan (look); the former represents the result of seeing, and the latter represents the action of looking. The eye was given prominence to express "see", using very artistic imagery.

祭 (🦵) (ji, offer sacrifice)

This character is composed of "示 (sacrificial altar)", "手, (hand)", and "肉, (meat)". It shows a hand placing a piece of meat on a sacrificial altar and offering it to the gods or ancestors as part of a ritual of worship. Common examples include "祭祀 jisi (sacrifice)", "拜祭 baiji (worship and sacrifice)," "祭奠 jidian (to hold a memorial ceremony for)," and "公祭 gongji (a public memorial service)."

盥 (🦵) (guan, to wash one's hands)

This is a drawing composed of "手 (hands)", "水 (water)", and "皿 (utensil)". It shows water between the pair of hands, and a basin containing water beneath them. "盥" means "to wash one's hands and face." On the door of public toilets in China, there are often signs that say "盥洗室 guanxishi." with "洗", meaning "wash" and "室" meaning "room".

艺 ( ) (yi, plant)

"艺yi" was originally an associative-compound character. In Jiaguwen (inscriptions on bones and tortoisehells), the character was composed of "人ren (person)" and "木mu (tree)": a person is kneeling on the ground and using both hands to plant a seedling, so the original meaning of "艺" is "plant". Planting trees correctly requires experience and technique, this meaning was later extended to cover a variety of other skills, such as "艺术yishu, art", "武术wushu, martial arts", and "美术meishu, fine arts". The simplified character "艺" became a pictophonetic character with "艹" as its form component and "乙" as its sound component.

祝 ( ) (zhu, pray)

In Jiaguwen, the character "祝" represented the act of sacrificing: it shows a person with a large head kneeling before a sacrificial altar, praying and offering sacrifice in hope of receiving a blessing from the gods. There are many common phrases composed of the character "祝", such as "祝贺 zhuhe (congratulate)", "祝福zhufu (bless)", "祝愿zhuyuan (wish)", "庆 祝qingzhu (celebrate)", and "敬祝jingzhu (wish)".

涉 ( ) (she, wade)

For the ancient character of "步bu (step)", we need to think of someone walking forward, one step at a time. The ancient character "涉she (wade)" shows a river running between two feet, which represents the act of wading across a river. The character "涉" means "to cross a river on foot".

灾 ( ) (zai, fire as a disaster)

This is one of the forms of the Jiaguwen character "灾", and is composed of "宀" and "火". It quite clearly depicts a house on fire. The modern simplified character has adopted the ancient form. Besides "fire" and "disaster", the character is used to express other catastrophes, such as flood, drought, hurricanes, plagues of insects, and the devastation caused by earthquakes.

牧 (𝖄) (mu, herd)

"牧" means "a herd of livestock." The ancient character "牧" is very interesting; it shows an ox in the foreground, and a hand behind it, driving the ox with a stick or branch (攴). It is a fascinating drawing of the act of herding, and other words that include "牧" have similar meanings, such as "放牧fangmu (herd)", "游牧youmu (nomadism)", "牧羊muyang (shepherd)", "牧马muma (the corralling of horses)", and "畜牧业xumuye (raising livestock)."

进 (𝖘) (jin, advance)

This is another example of an associative-compound character, and reflects the ancient people's strong visual awareness. In Jiaguwen, the character "进" has a bird (the character "隹") at the top, and a foot (the character 止) beneath it, indicating a bird walking or hopping forward on the ground. A bird can only move forward, not backwards, so this character means "advance". Later "止" became "辶", and this is the complex character "進". It has now been simplified to the pictophonetic character "进".

休 (𝖎𝖝) (xiu, have a rest)

This is composed of "人ren (person)" and "木mu (tree)". It shows a person who is tired and so leans against a tree, indicating the act of taking a rest. It provides a miniature portrait of the daily life of the outdoor laborer, back in ancient times. This character appears in the common phrases "休息 xiuxi (rest)", "休闲xiuxian (rest and recreation at leisure time)", "休假xiujia (vacation)", "休整xiuzheng (rest and consolidation)", and "退休tuixiu (retire)."

相 (𝖝𝖔) (xiang, mutually)

This character shows an eye staring at a tree directly in front of it, and means observation and mutuality. In a poem by Li Bai, a great poet during the Tang Dynasty (618-907 AD),is a verse that reads "相看两不厌，只有敬亭山 (We are not tired of gazing at each other, and there is only the Jingtingshan Mountain)." This means that the poet and the mountain intensely regard each other, and so the mountain in the poem is invested with human feeling.

寒 (image) (han, cold)

This character is composed of "宀(屋) (house)", "(草) (grass)", "人 (person)", and "冫(冰) (ice)". It shows a man crouching on the grass inside his house, and ice on the ground, which gives the impression of cold. In modern Chinese, many phrases indicating extreme cold include the character "寒", such as "寒冷hanleng (very cold)", "寒风hanfeng (cold wind)", "严寒yanhan (chilliness)", "寒假hanjia (winter vacation)", and "天寒地冻tianhandidong (the weather is cold and there is ice on the ground)".

津 (image) (jin, ferry)

The character "津jin" means ferry. In Jiaguwen, the character is actually an illustration of a ferry, showing a boatman standing at the back of a boat, and punting it with a pole in order to cross the river. The component "舟(船) (boat)", was later dropped from the character, and it became a simpler combination of "河水(氵) (river)" and "竿(聿) (pole)" Its meaning, though, is still very clear. A big Chinese city, "天津Tianjin" actually means "the ferry of the son of heaven (emperor)". In the Ming Dynasty (1368 - 1644) during the war for the throne, General Yongle led his forces to victory in a battle after crossing the river in Tianjin. He subsequently became Emperor, and so the city received its current name, "天津Tianjin".

梦 (H 夕) (meng, dream)

This is a very interesting character. In Jiaguwen, it depicted a man lying in bed and having a dream, and showed him opening his eyes very widely and raising his eyebrows, as though he had "seen" something in his sleep. The component "床 bed" was later omitted from the character, and "夕" was added, indicating evening. The eyebrows were also altered. Today's simplified character is "梦", and none of its components illustrate a person having a dream.

逐 (image) (zhu, chase)

This character means "chase". In ancient times it had a very creative formation, showing a wild boar (the character "豕") running, and being followed by a foot ("character "止") of a person, indicating a hunter chasing a wild boar. Later the character "止" changed to the form component "辶", indicating "walk".

朝 (𣴎) (zhāo, morning)

This character means "morning". Its ancient form had "木mu (tree)" on its left side, and "日 ri (sun)" above and below, indicating that the sun had just risen from the east and had not yet risen above the trees. On the right was "月yue (moon)", indicating that the moon was still visible in the west. This is believed to represent dawn, when the sun and the moon can both be seen in the sky.

莫 (𦱴) (mo, don't)

In ancient times the character (mù) indicated the sunset. It vividly illustrates the scene at sunset, with the sun going down over a stretch of grass and shown very low in the sky, indicating that the day is drawing to a close and the evening will soon begin. It has now become the character "暮(mù)", which indicates the meaning of sunset, because the earlier character "莫" was loaned to represent "don't." In order to differentiate the two meanings, the character "日ri (sun)" was added below the character "莫". The new character, "暮", that resulted, now indicates the sunset.

The meanings of different-compound characters come from the combination of their separate parts. For example, "小xiao (small)" and "大da (big)" form the character "尖jian (sharp)", and "上shang (up)" and "下xia (down)" combine to produce "卡ka (get stuck)". Other different-compound characters express meaning by directly repeating the compounds, for example, "小土xiaotu (small earth)" forms "尘chen (dust)", "小鸟xiaoniao (small bird)" forms "雀que (sparrow)", "不正buzheng (not central)" forms "歪wai (devious)", "不好buhao (not good)" forms "孬nao (bad)", "不用buyong (do not)" forms "甭beng (don't)", "山石shanshi (mountain stone)" forms "岩yan (rock)", "山高shangao (high mountain)" forms "嵩song (lofty)", "大力dali (great power)" forms "夯hang (ram)". A development of "手shou (hand)" forms "拜bai (bow, pray)", whereas a separation of "手shou (hand)" forms "掰bai (break off)".

It is also worth noting that among the simplified characters, there are also many associative-compound characters, also created with the skill of combination. For example, "泪lei (tear)" actually looks like an eye with a tear running from it, and "笔bi (pen)" illustrates a brush pen with a bamboo stem and a bristle tip. Other simplified characters, such as "灶zao (kitchen range)", "双shuang (double)", "对dui (answer)", "尘chen (dust)", "体ti (body)", "国guo (state)", "孙sun (grandson)", "宝bao (treasure)", "帘lian (curtain)", "阴yin (shade)", "阳yang (bright)", and "盖gai (cover)" are all new associative-compound characters - all the result of the skilful combination of existing characters - and some are derived from ancient forms. In short, the formation of associative-compound characters represents not just meaning, but also the thought and wisdom of the Chinese people.

Combining Pronunciation and Form: Pictophonetic Characters

A pictophonetic character is a composed of a form component (a drawing), which indicates

文字 (wen-zi, characters): In ancient times "文" and "字" represented two different concepts. Ancient philologists called independent characters without a component "文" (for example pictographic and indicative characters), and called combined characters with components "字" (associative-compound and pictophonetic characters). "文" and "字" broadly reflected two developing stages of the Han characters - pure ideogram, and a combination of ideogram and phonogram. In the *Shuowen Jiezi*, Xu Shen said, "in early times, when Cang Jie created characters, pictographic characters were known as '文'. Later there appeared a combination of forms and sounds, and the characters thus created were called '字'. Characters of '文' are the origin of things, and the characters shown as '字' are the multiplication of those things. There are many such characters." This passage explains the idea of two different concepts. Today, "文字" has become a disyllabic noun, and both independent and combined characters are called "文字".

meaning, and a sound component, which indicates pronunciation. In the other types of character, the components indicate only meaning. By incorporating pronunciation as well as meaning, the pictophonetic characters broke new ground. Many more characters could be formed using the pictophonetic method, so it became the main way of forming characters. Today more than 80 percent of the Han characters, and 70 percent of common characters, are pictophonetic. They are also known as "characters of combination."

Marking Sounds onto Drawings. Only a few characters could be formed using pictographic, indication and associative-compound methods, because it was impossible to depend only on the association of form and meaning. It is difficult, for example, to form the character "湖hu (lake)" by using the above three methods; however, when we employ the pictophonetic method, it becomes easier. In the pictophonetic method, "氵 水 (water)" is used as the form component, to indicate something of which water is a part (the ancient character form of "氵" is a drawing of running water), and a ready-made character "胡" was added as the sound component to indicate its pronunciation, resulting in the character "湖". By adding this sound component to other characters with a different pronunciation, more characters relating to water can be created.

Form Component	Sound Component	Han Character
氵	胡(hú)	湖(hú)
氵	青(qīng)	清(qīng)
氵	州(zhōu)	洲(zhōu)
氵	肖(xiāo)	消(xiāo)
氵	气(qì)	汽(qì)
氵	农(nóng)	浓(nóng)
氵	林(lín)	淋(lín)
氵	干(gān)	汗(hàn)
氵	羊(yáng)	洋(yáng)

The First Method of Forming of Pictophonetic Characters: Form Component + Sound Component

Sound Component	Form Component	Han Character
包(bāo)	扌	抱(bào)
包(bāo)	月	胞(bāo)
包(bāo)	饣	饱(bǎo)
包(bāo)	氵	泡(pào)
包(bāo)	足	跑(pǎo)
包(bāo)	衤	袍(páo)
包(bāo)	火	炮(pào)
包(bāo)	刂	刨(bào)
包(bāo)	艹	苞(bāo)

The Second Method of Forming of Pictophonetic Characters: Sound Component + Form Component

Matching Sounds with Drawings. By matching characters that indicate pronunciation (sound components) with characters of various different meanings (form components), we can create a wide range of pictophonetic characters with the same, or similar, pronunciation. For example, the character "包 bāo" is a sound component, and many pictophonetic characters with the same or a similar pronunciations can be formed from it, such as "抱 bào (hold in one's arms)", "苞 bāo (bud)", and "跑 pǎo (run)."

The Structure of Pictophonetic Characters. There are six ways of combining the sound and form components of pictophonetic characters: form on the left and sound on the right; form on the right and sound on the left; form above and sound below; form below and sound above; form on the outside and sound on the inside; and form on the inside and sound on the outside. Most characters have the first structure, with form on the left and sound on the right, although "form above and sound below" characters are also frequently used.

Pictographic characters still appear amongst the simplified Han characters today. Among the modern simplified Han characters there are many new pictophonetic characters that have a concise form, an exact pronunciation, and a definite meaning. For example, "拥 yong (embrace)", "护 hu (protect)", "担 dan (carry on a shoulder pole)", "拦 lan (hold back)", "栏 lan (railing)", "战 zhan (battle)", "惊 jing (be frightened)", "响 xiang (echo)", "吓 xia (scare)", "虾 xia (shrimp)", "态 tai (attitude)", "忆 yi (recall)", "艺 yi (plant)", "攻 gong (attack)", "疗 liao (cure)", and "园 yuan (garden)" are all new pictophonetic characters that have been successfully simplified.

The Function of the Characters: Indicating Meaning. Pictophonetic characters represent an advanced method of formation. This method has progressed a long way from drawings, which only used form to indicate meaning, and has greatly increased the number of Han characters. As a result, pictophonetic characters now represent the majority of Han characters. They have components indicating sound, which implies that they developed phonographically, but they are basically a system of ideographic characters. The pictophonetic characters are composed of ideographic components, which indicate meaning, and sound components - graphic characters that are

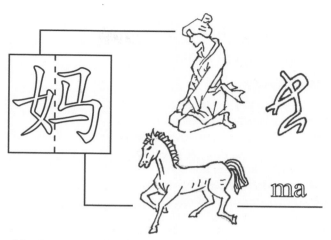

Formation of the character "妈ma (mother)".
In the character "妈ma (mother)", the form component "女nu (female)" is a pictographic character, indicating that "妈妈mama (mother)" is female, and the sound component "马 ma (horse)" was loaned to indicate the pronunciation. It was originally a pictographic character indicating "horse".

used to indicate pronunciation. For example, in the pictophonetic character "妈ma (mother)", "马ma (horse)" is a pictographic character, and in the character "淋lin (drench)", "林lin (woods)" is a graphic associative-compound character, and the component "木mu (tree)" is a pictographic character.

Han characters also include many pictographic, indicative, and associative-compound characters that directly use form to indicate meaning. The frequent appearance of pictophonetic characters extended the graphic components' use, and strengthened their ability to indicate meaning. When the Han characters became pictophonetic, then, their graphic quality became more prominent. This answers the question of why there are such a large number of pictophonetic characters in the Han system, whose form components have a strong graphic function, and also tells us why the Han characters did not develop into phonograms.

After a long period of evolution, the sound components we see today, which consist of many pictophonetic characters, do not represent the exact pronunciation. It is worth bearing this in mind when we are learning and using them.

Mutual Explanation: Mutually Explanatory Characters

Mutually explanatory characters represent a particular kind of formation within the ancient "six categories." It refers to a group of characters that have the same components, same meanings, and similar pronunciations. In the *Shuowen Jiezi*, the author used the two characters "老 lao (old)" and "考 kao (aged)" as examples of this. Both characters incorporate the component "老 lao (old)" and they have similar pronunciations and the same meaning. Mutually

A page explaining the character 老 lao (old):, in *The Annotation of the Shuowen Jiezi*.

explanatory characters like these came into being because different speakers, from different regions, used different dialects. However while the term "mutually explanatory" is an effective way of explaining one ancient character by reference to another, it does not describe a method of formation. For example, "老 lao (old)" is an associative-compound character and "考 kao (aged)" is a pictophonetic character, and neither is newly created. Other mutually explanatory characters include "顶 dǐng (top)" and "颠 diān (top)", "芳 fāng (fragrant)" and "芬 fēn (fragrant)", "绩 jì (twist hemp thread)", and "绩 jī (twisted hemp thread)".

Substituting the Same Sound: Phonetic Loan Characters

Phonetic loan characters were important in the development of the Han characters. In linguistic terms, they use a ready-made character to create a new character that is a homophone of it (a similar pronunciation).

It is difficult to create a new character for every new Chinese word, and the simplest way to resolve this is to borrow another character. For example, the associative-compound character "北

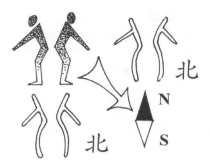

The character "北bei", expressing the meaning of "opposition", was loaned to indicate the direction of north "北bei".

The character "月yue" was added to the character "北", to form the character "背bei", indicating the original meaning of "opposition"

bei" looks like two people standing back-to-back, and its original meaning was "opposition" or "violation." There had previously been no character representing the meaning of direction. Because it had the same pronunciation, the associative-compound character "北bei" was conveniently borrowed to represent the direction of North. Today the original meaning of the character has disappeared, and as a phonetic loan character, it is only used to represent the compass direction of North. Phonetic loan characters make use of the substitution of the same sound; in other words, they only borrow the sound (which naturally includes the form) of a ready-made character, and their meaning is superfluous. However, thanks to these practical phonetic loan characters, which came about because there were not enough characters to represent the whole language, many Chinese words that were difficult to create characters for, have been preserved. Phonetic loan characters, then, were crucially important in the historical development of the Han characters.

During the Shang and Zhou Dynasties, when the number of characters was small, many phonetic loan characters emerged, inscribed onto tortoiseshells, and represented all of the characters in the language. Therefore we can definitely say that the period of Jiaguwen was also the age of the creation of phonetic loan characters.

When a character was loaned to express a new meaning, it resulted in one character coming to have several meanings. For example, when the character "北bei" became a phonetic loan character, it could either mean opposition and violation, or the new, loaned meaning of a direction. In order to resolve this problem, and differentiate between the meaning of a loaned character and its original meaning, it was necessary to create another character to express its original meaning. For example, the form component "月(肉)(flesh)", meaning "body", was added to the character "北", and the character "背" was created to express the original meaning. Adding a component, then, resolves the problem posed by phonetic loan characters, and results in the formation of new pictophonetic characters. Most pictophonetic characters were formed in this way, resulting in a large number of new pictophonetic characters. It was unanticipated that phonetic loan characters would make such a contribution to the Han characters' development.

Phonetic loan characters became, and continue to be, a mainstream method for forming characters. Just as in ancient times, a large number of phonetic loan characters are still in everyday use.

甲	乙	丙	丁	东	西	南	北	之	乎	者	也
而	其	要	莫	亦	勿	七	九	豆	何	止	我
来	易	都	会	能	骄	求	又	花	自	难	它
应该	可以	咖啡	纽约	丁冬	光当	哗拉	滴答				

The Form and Structure of the Modern Han Characters

The form and structure of Han characters are composed on several levels, and there is a prescribed order in which they should be written, which makes them easy to write. The Chinese people are as adept at it as they are at using chopsticks. Modern Han characters are square and composed of strokes, and their form and structure has three levels: stroke, component, and character. Of these, the component is at the core of the character's structure.

Basic Stroke	Name	Category	Name	Example
丶	Dot	丶	斜点	主、下
		ノ	左点	小、办
一	Horizontal stroke	一	长横	十、下
		一	短横	士、未
丨	Vertical stroke	丨	长竖	丰、上
		丨	短竖	列、止
ノ	Left-falling stroke	ノ	平撇	乎、千
		ノ	竖撇	风、片
丶	Right-falling stroke	乀	斜捺	八、文
		一	平捺	之、这
㇕	Turning sroke	㇕	横折	国、五
		ㄴ	竖折	区、母
㇏	Lifting stroke	㇀	斜提	打、习
		㇀	竖提	比、饭
㇄	Hook stroke	㇆	横钩	买、军
		亅	竖钩	小、可
		㇄	竖弯钩	七、儿

The major strokes of the Han Characters

Strokes and their Order

Strokes are the various dots and lines of which the Han characters are composed. In writing, a stroke begins as soon as the pen touches the paper, and is completed when it is raised. There are eight basic strokes in Han characters: dots, horizontal strokes, vertical strokes, left-falling strokes, right-falling strokes, turning strokes, lifting strokes, and hook strokes. These strokes also have variants. For example, vertical strokes can be short or long, and there are also vertical left-falling strokes, vertical turning strokes, vertical lifting strokes, vertical hook strokes, vertical turning hooks, and so forth. Han characters are composed of basic strokes and their variants. Modern Han characters have a square form. There are no round strokes, and very few arcs.

Independent Characters	Combined Characters	Independent Characters	Combined Characters
土	城、场	王	理、现
月	请、清	车	辆、轿
木	林、松	火	灯、烧
禾	秋、稻	又	欢、对
七	切	己	改
半	叛	足	跑

Illustration of changes in strokes. These independent characters change when they serve as left-side components, in order to maintain formal balance be easily written.

Only the left-falling and right-falling strokes are slightly curved; the rest are basically straight. For example, the sun is round, but the character "日ri (sun)" is square and composed of straight strokes. Of all of the strokes, horizontal and vertical strokes predominate, and being able to reproduce them is a basic requirement for writing Han characters. The strokes of each standard Han character have a fixed number, form and position, which cannot be changed.

So that the forms of the Han characters are balanced, aesthetic, and easy to write, some changes to the strokes are allowed. For example in the left component, when the last stroke is a horizontal stroke, it changes to a lifting stroke, as in the characters "地di (earth)", "现xian (appear)", "轮lun (wheel)", and "孩hai (child)". In the left component, when the last stroke is a right-falling stroke, it changes to a dot, as in the characters "林lin (woods)", "灯deng (lamp)", "利li (sharp)", and "剩sheng (remnant)". When "月yue (moon)" is a component in the lower part of a character, the first vertical left-falling stroke becomes a vertical stroke, as in the characters "青qing (blue)", "前qian (front)", "能neng (ability)", and "谓wei (tell)". These changes to the strokes must be remembered when we learn to write Han characters.

The Order of the Strokes. The strokes of the Han characters must be drawn in a specific order, as follows: a horizontal stroke comes before a vertical one (十shi, ten), a left-falling stroke comes before a right-falling one (人ren, person), an upper stroke comes before a lower one (二er, two), a left stroke comes before a right one (川chuan, river), an outer part comes before an inner part (月yue, moon), a central stroke comes before those on either side of it (小),

> *The order of strokes must be*
> *followed, and the pen will gain*
> *strength from this.*
> *Horizontal, vertical, up and down,*
> *And left-falling prior to right-*
> *Falling strokes on the left and the*
> *Right respectively.*
> *Write the center before the two*
> *Outer sides, and make the center*
> *Bold and decisive.*
> *Don't forget to write the outer*
> *Part before the inner part, and*
> *Remember that phrase about*
> *entering the house before closing*
> *the door.*

The Song *Orders of Strokes*

and finally, we must formulate what we can best describe as "entering before closing the door". Writing Han characters in the prescribed order not only means we can write them quickly and correctly, but also helps us to understand their structure. Strokes that have not been written in the correct order are called "inverted strokes." They will have been written quickly, and their writers will not have properly grasped their structure. For example, when writing the character "进 jin (enter)", "井" should be written before "辶", so that the pen is in the correct place to begin the next stroke.

Components

Generally speaking, we call components "偏旁 piān páng" meaning "composed of strokes." Components are the basic parts from which the Han characters are formed, being bigger than strokes, but smaller than characters. There are two types of component: character components (independent characters), and non-character components (variants of independent characters). In modern combined characters, each part is a component. For example the character "好 hao (good)" is composed of "女 nu (female)" and "子 zi (baby)", both of which are character components. The character "谢 xie (thank)" is composed of three components: a non-character component "讠" and two character components, "身 shen (body)" and "寸 cun (1\3 decimeter)". The components of "衫 shan (sleeveless jacket)" are "衤" and "彡" which are both non-character components.

77

Index of Radicals
Page numbers to the right of the radicals

One stroke		人(入)	18	厶	21	口	27	⼹(彐彑)		歹	41	气	43
一	14	勹	18	又(ㄡ)	21	囗	29		35	车(車)	41	攵	43
丨	15	勹(见刀)		廴	21	巾	29	尸	35	戈	41	片	43
丿	15	儿	18	巳(见卩)		山	29	己(巳)	36	比	41	斤	43
丶	15	几(几)	18	Three strokes		彳	30	弓	36	瓦	41	爪(爫)	44
乙(一乛		亠	18	工	21	彡	30	屮	36	止	41	父	44
乚)	15	冫	19	土	21	犭	30	女	36	攴	42	月(⺼)	44
Two strokes		冖	19	士	22	夕	31	子(孑)	37	小(见忄)		欠	45
二	15	讠(言)	19	艹	22	夂	31	纟(糸)	37	日	42	风(風)	45
十	15	卩(㔾)	20	廾(在下)		饣(食)	31	马(馬)	38	日(曰)	42	殳	45
厂	16	阝(在左)			24	丬(爿)	31	幺	38	水(氺)	42	文	45
匚	16		20	大	24	广	31	巛	38	贝(貝)	42	方	45
卜(⺊)	16	阝(在右)		尢	25	门(門)	31	Four strokes		见(見)	43	火	45
刂	16		20	扌	25	氵	32	王	38	牛(牜牛)	43	斗	46
冂	16	凵	21	寸	26	忄(⺗)	34	韦(韋)	39		43	灬	46
亻	16	刀(⺈)	21	弋	26	宀	34	木	39	手	43	户	46
八(丷)	18	力	21	小(⺌)	26	辶(辶)	35	犬	41	毛	43	礻(⺬)	46

Index of Radicals in *Hanyu Cidian (Chinese Dictionary)*

More than 1,000 years ago, Xu Shen's *Shuowen Jiezi* (*Origin of Chinese Characters*), analyzed the forms of the Han characters in terms of their components. Independent characters were the first type of character to be created, and in turn they were used to create combined characters, so independent characters are actually constituent parts of the combined ones. Knowing their components is very useful when looking up characters in a dictionary. Today, the Han characters have been successfully incorporated into computer software on the basis of their component structure.

Radicals

Xu Shen described the components of characters in terms of "radicals". He classified the components into categories, with the first listed component in a character being its radical, such as "木 mu (tree)" and "人 ren (person)". All the characters in the category with the radical "木 mu (tree)" have the component of "木", and all the characters in the category with the radical "人" have the component "人". To put it simply, a radical is the "head of a category." All radicals are components, but not all components are radicals; for example, the sound component of a pictophonetic character is

人(亻)、子、女、足、页、目、口
耳、月、手(扌)、舌、衣(衤)、又
水(氵)、贝、车、舟、马、木、止
疒、皿、火(灬)、心(忄)、纟、鸟
宀、土、山、石、气、示(礻)、虫
门、彳、立、钅、讠、巾、广、雨
王(玉)、米、酉、鱼、立、禾、牛

Radicals in Han Characters are ideographic form components.

a component, but it is not a radical because it just indicates the characters' pronunciation. Most radicals are ideographic form components. It is easiest to look up words in a dictionary on the basis of radicals.

A radical represents a large category, and dictionaries usually contain more than 200 radicals, across more than 200 categories. Each category includes many specific things, so 200 radicals can form the basis of thousands of Han characters. For example, we can find the names of trees, various parts of trees, and wood products, all under the radical "木 mu (tree)".

Whole Characters

Whole characters are in common use, and are composed of several parts, using a combination of form, pronunciation, and meaning. Whole characters are divided into single-part characters (independent characters), and multi-part characters (combined characters). Among the modern Han characters, there are only a few single-part characters, representing less than ten percent of the overall total. The other 90+ percent are multi-part characters. Of these, the majority are composed of three parts, and these account for over 40 percent of the total characters.

Single-part characters have only one part and are independent. There are not many independent characters, but the ones that exist are in common use and have an important function in the formation of other characters.

CHINESE CHARACTERS

人	木	水	土	山
心	目	女	子	鸟
羊	牛	犬	马	贝

左右结构	休 汗 跑 唱 棵
上下结构	花 竿 架 爸 空
包围结构	园 围 问 闻 辨

Single-part characters are independent characters.

Multi-part characters are combined characters.

Multi-part characters and combined characters are composed of two or more parts. They can be either a combination of independent characters, or a combination of independent characters and components that have been changed from independent characters, such as "明 ming (bright)" and "森 sen (forest)" for the former category, and "抱 bao (hold in arms)" and "笔 bi (pen)" in the latter.

Combined characters form the majority of characters, and principally have three structures: left and right, up and down, and encircled. Most of them are composed of left and right parts.

Learning the formation of Han characters involves learning their form and structure. Pictographic characters are based on form and structure, a major reason why the Han characters still have a strong ideographic quality. Although, as previously mentioned, Han characters are ideographic, most of them indicate both meaning and pronunciation. In terms of formation and usage, the ideogram is their most notable feature.

The Profound Mystery of the Han Characters

Han characters typically have a square form. The Chinese people deliberately chose this form when they first created the characters, due to the ideogram and the independence of Chinese pronunciation.

Han characters are visual forms, and their square formation satisfies the basic requirement that they are perceived as stable and consistent. The forms of the characters are somewhat mysterious.

The mysteries of the Han characters are mostly hidden in their pictographic strokes. Modern characters no longer look like drawings, but their pictographic elements are reminiscent of them.

Why the Han Characters have Square Forms

Han characters use form to indicate meaning, and a square form is the most convenient way to achieve this. Square forms occupy a two-dimensional space and provide scope for a sufficient amount of content. There are various combinations of strokes that are written up and down, and left and right, and creating them within a square formation is the easiest way to achieve symmetry and visual balance. Because of this, all Han characters developed in a square form.

Natural Selection in the Aspect of Vision

When the characters were first created, it seems that the ancient Chinese people quite deliberately chose the square form, as the numerous primitive rock paintings, symbols carved onto pottery, and early characters, were almost all square. The earliest character, the symbol of "旦" from the Dawenkou Culture, was obviously a rectangle, and the earliest mature characters, i.e. the Jiaguwen and Jinwen characters, almost all had rectangular forms. Xiaozhuan characters, standardized by Emperor Qinshihuang of the Qin Dynasty (221-206 BC) were rectangular, with symmetry between top and bottom and left and right. After the change to Lishu, the Han characters were gradually fixed into a square form, and today's Kaishu characters have a very regular square form. So we can definitely say that the square form is a fundamental feature of the Han characters, and that their evolution has progressed from an irregular to a regular square form. The square form of the Han characters came about as a result of natural selection, based on visual appeal.

Modern Buildings with a Square Shape

The Character "来lai (come)" in a "米"-shaped Pane
The major strokes of the character "米" clearly accord with the axis of the 米"-shaped pane, giving it visual stability.

The Balance of Structure in the 米"-shaped Pane
In the character "扮ban (to be dressed up as)", the left part is small while the right part is large, but in the square form both the left and right sides attain balance. This is what we refer to as "visual balance." It is a kind of visual impression, and characters with visual balance exhibit beauty and stability.

In terms of visual appeal, the square form gives the impression of stability, because it has an immediately apparent central point. The center is the most stable place, and is a balancing point of force, so a character would lose its sense of balance if it deviated from it. The central point has a focal force that applies to all of the strokes inside the square form, so that the strokes all close in on the center, and achieve a balance of forces. The practice of writing Han characters inside the "米mi (rice)"- shaped panes, illustrates this point. The central point of a "米"-shaped pane intersects at a point of four axes. The central point and the four axes are all in comparatively stable positions, and the major strokes of Han characters must accord at least approximately with theses axes, in order to achieve stability. For example, the major strokes of the character "水shui (water)" fundamentally accord with the axes, making the whole character appear stable. If the character "水" is used as a component, the three strokes of "three-point 水" are also all directed towards the center point.

In order to achieve the desired visual balance, the strokes on both sides, or over and above the "十" axis, must also all be basically symmetrical. For example, "水shui (water)", "木mu (tree)", "林lin (woods)", and "扮ban (to be dressed up as)" are equally symmetrical from left to right, and "显xian (apparent)", "安an (safety)", "胃wei (stomach)", and "呂lu" are equally symmetrical from top to bottom, and they all create the visual impression of stability. Although the right and left strokes, and those that go up and down, do not cover the exact same area, the result is still a visual balance.

When we look at a square form, the lower or right part is intuitively bigger, heavier, and more stable, so the Han characters with the most stable structure are usually those that are smaller at the top and wider at the bottom, or smaller on the left-hand side and bigger on the right-hand side.

The Imperial Palace in Beijing
The Imperial Palace is often thought of as foursquare, which means that there are axes in its planar layout and the buildings on either side are roughly symmetrical. Therefore when people look at it they will get a sense of stability. This is similar to the square form of the Han characters.

The Decisive Role of the Ideogram

With their origin in drawings, Han characters are graphic, and their fundamental function is to convey meaning through visual form. Their form components – pictographic, indicative, associative-compound and pictophonetic – all indicate meaning through visual form, and the sound component of a pictophonetic character is an additional loaned form. It can be said that the aim of the Han characters is to transform meaning into a visual and understandable form. For example, characters such as "休xiu (rest)", "花hua (flower)", "晶jing (brilliant)", "国guo (country)", and "餐can (meal)" all represent the spatial combination of strokes and components. Without a two-dimensional canvas of left and right, and up and down, it would be impossible to form as many different Han characters as there are. Alphabetic writing is different, because it only indicates pronunciation and has no relation to meaning, so its form is very simple and space is not an issue. Words composed of alphabetic letters are also in linear order, so they do not need to use a square space. For example the English word "dragon" is a linear arrangement of six alphabetic letters, whereas the corresponding Han character, "龙long" began as a drawing of a dragon. It later

The square character "龙(龙)long (dragon)". Since ancient times the drawing-like character "龙" has occupied a square space. It is quite different from the English word "dragon," which has a linear structure.

became a combination of strokes, which all required a square space. Therefore the ideographs that developed into the Han characters needed to occupy a geometrical area, in which they could achieve visual balance in order to create meaning.

Square characters are very well-suited to the nature of Chinese, as the language has many dialects and a large number of homonyms. Han characters indicate meaning through visual form, rather than representing an auditory sound. Chinese people from different parts of the country, and from different ethnic groups, can all understand the meanings of the square characters, because they all express meaning visually. Linear writing would not be practical for Chinese; for example the Mandarin sentence "又有油，又有肉 (there is both oil and meat)" would be pronounced as "you you you, you you you" in the Shandong dialect, which would be nonsensical; however expressing it in six visual squares means that it can be understood anywhere in the country.

The Independence of Syllables

Han characters are the basic structural units for recording the Chinese language, and represent a combination of pronunciation and meaning. Generally speaking, a character records one syllable, a syllable represents one morpheme, and each syllable corresponds to a character. For example, the character "书" represents the syllable "shu", and that syllable in turn represents the morpheme "书 (book)". The Han characters are highly suited to the nature of Chinese; for example the sentence "我们学习汉语 wo-men-xue-xi-han-yu (we learn Chinese)" consists of six syllables represented by six characters. One character records one syllable, and each syllable is a character. The syllables of the Chinese language are independent and cannot be combined with other syllables. Each character is also independent and cannot be transformed into another character. The independence of the Chinese syllables, then, is the reason why Han characters correspond to syllables, and have taken on independent square forms.

Perspective in the Han Characters

The Han characters are based on pictographic characters, and are graphic with a combination of form, pronunciation, and meaning. Due to the evolution of the strokes and their consequent simplification, modern Han characters are no longer pictographic, but they do contain some remnants of the ancient pictographic characters and their strokes and symbols still express meaning. The pictographic elements of the Han characters are also very helpful in their study and use.

Pictographic Elements in Independent Characters

Among the Han characters not many are independent, and those that are are almost all pictographic characters. To begin with they were all pictorgraphic; for example the ancient form of the character "日 ri (sun)" was a rounded sun, "山 shan (mountain)" was a literal painting of three peaks, "水 shui (water)" looked like a flowing river, "人 ren (person)" was a profile of a person with arms outstretched, and "手 shou (hand)" showed the shape of a hand with five fingers. We no longer find such vivid drawings in the modern Han characters, but the basic shapes of the original drawings are still visible. The character "日" has been changed from a round sun to a square sun, and the three peaks of "山" have been simplified into three vertical strokes.

The table on the next page shows the pictographic elements within the modern Han characters.

Pictographic elements in the character "马 ma (horse)"
"馬", the complex form of "马", evolved from the ancient character, which resembled a drawing. In the complex form "馬", the three horizontal strokes in the upper part depict the long hair on a horse's neck, the four dots in the lower part are its legs, and the horizontal, vertical and turning strokes in the middle represent the head, body and tail. We can even see the horse's eyes.

Independent Characters	Ancient Character Forms	Drawings of Characters' Origin	Analysis of Pictographic Elements
日 Sun			The rounded line of the ancient character of "日ri (sun)" gradually became the strokes of "口kou(mouth)" in the modern character, and the horizontal stroke in "日" was originally a dot in a circle.
山 Mountain			The three vertical strokes were originally three peaks in the ancient character of "山 shan (mountain)".
木 Tree			The vertical stroke was the trunk of the ancient character "木mu (tree)", the horizontal stroke was the branch, and the left-falling and right-falling strokes were the roots.
禾 Grain			"木mu (tree)" indicates plant, and the left-falling stroke is the ear of the plant.
女 Female			The first and second strokes represent crossed arms and the horizontal stroke is the body.
母 Mother			The frame of the character is the variant of the ancient character "女nu (female)", the horizontal stroke in the middle is the body and the two dots inside represent her breasts.
子 Child			The horizontal turning stroke in the upper part is the exaggerated head of the ancient character "子zi(child)", the vertical hook stroke indicates the body and one leg and the horizontal stroke represents the arms.
手 Hand			The left-falling stroke and two horizontal strokes indicate five fingers.
鱼 (魚) Fish			(A complex character) The upper part is the fish's head, "田tian(field)" is the fish's body, and the four dots are its tail.
马 (馬) Horse			(A complex character) The three horizontal strokes above are the long mane on the horse's neck, the four dots below are its legs, and the horizontal, vertical and turning strokes in the middle represent the head, body and tail of the horse.

Independent Characters	Ancient Character Forms	Drawings of Characters' Origin	Analysis of Pictographic Elements
鼠 Mouse			"臼jiu(mortar)" is a mouse. It has the protruding teeth of a mouse, the strokes in the lower right part indicate the mouse's feet, and the last long stroke indicates the mouse's body and tail.
象 Elephant			The stroke "⼑" is the trunk of an elephant, "⼝" is the elephant's head, the stroke in the lower middle part is the body, the stroke on the left is the leg, and the last stroke, the right-falling stroke, is the tail.
龙 (龍) Dragon			(A complex character) The left part is the dragon's head, "立li(stand)" is the dragon's horns, "月yue(month)" is an open mouth with sharp teeth, and the right bent stroke is the body and tail of the dragon.
车 (車) chariot			(A complex character) The vertical stroke is the vehicle axle, the "田tian(field)" in the middle is the wheels, and the two horizontal strokes above and below are the peg locking up the vehicle.
衣 clothes			The horizontal, left-falling and right-falling strokes compose two sleeves, and the vertical hook and short left-falling strokes are the lower hem of the clothes.

In the Han writing system, many independent characters are similar in shape, such as "木mu (tree)" and "禾he (ripened grain)." The difference between the two characters is only in a horizontal left-falling stroke on "木", a pictographic stroke that is used purely for differentiating the two characters.. "禾" represents a grain with an ear, the horizontal left-falling stroke depicting the ear itself.

Because independent characters have a definite meaning and a strong ideographic function, most of them have become radicals of combined characters. For example, "日" means both the sun and time, and all combined characters that have "日" as their radical represent these meanings, such as "明ming (bright)", "时shi (time)", "晚wan (evening)", "昨zuo (yesterday)", and "旱han (drought)". The independent characters that serve as radicals have fewer strokes and

业部										1193			765	(胭)	967
		瞀	1545	睨	925	矇	869								
		眃	1427	睢	1208	(矓)	868	五至六画				(疊)	292	(𦥎)	834
业	1468	眽	876	睥	968	𥉑	686	(𤑳)	69					阃	687
邺	1470	眙	171	眿	117		1045	畐	1249	罒部					
凿	1571		1484	脻	1210	(䀹)	617	𤰞	1290	四	1196	皿部			
黹	1620	眶	736	(脮)	688	譛	1581	(眹)	1280	三至八画		罒	885		
(睾)	1468	眭	1208	(暖)	1101	睦	822	唸	1600	罗	834	三至五画			
黻	389	眦	1672	睘	825	(鼪)	817	留	809	罘	387	盂	1534		
(鼗)	212	(㫳)	1672	九至十画		(黱)	706	(畞)	901	罚	341	盅	870		
誩	392	眅	898	瞀	1081	(黉)	1644	畜	190	罝	413	(盃)	51
		眺	1253	睒	180				1422	罚	20	(盇)	512
目部		眵	167	睚	1202	田部			950	(罘)	21	盐	1631
		眙	1603	睴	525	田	1248	畔	61	罟	452	盆	959
目	903	眩	176	(䁐)	871	甲	607	畟	996	罡	680	盈	1510
二至四画		眷	688		872	申	1118	畤	1624	罦	448	盍	1582
盯	293	眛	871	睑	819	由	1521	(畁)	1492	(師)	814	盐	1447
盱	1419		872	睽	738	电	282	略	831	罧	460	盎	512
盲	853	眼	1449	普	859	二至三画		(罢)	831	(畀)	846	盦	95
相	1371	眸	900	睦	712	町	293	累	764	胃	688	盟	614
	1377	睐	1101	瞒	849		1259		765	罴	389		622
眍	723	眯	749	瞢	869	毗	710		766	罶	781	盒	12
眄	877	眴	1113	瞌	152	畄	743	七画以上		羀	1173	盗	512
	880														

Hanyu Cidian (*Chinese Dictionary*) includes independent characters that serve as radicals, in its index of radicals.

an important role in forming other characters. They also have fixed meanings and pronunciations, and their pictographic elements are more obvious than those of other characters. More than 90 per cent of the modern Han characters are composed of radicals. In order to learn and use Han characters correctly, we first need a thorough knowledge of radicals, from which we can then learn a large number of characters. In order to recognize and learn written Han language, it is very important to grasp independent characters.

Pictographic Elements in Combined Characters

A combined character has several parts, such as "明ming (bright)", "妈ma (mother)", "河he (river)", "把ba (hold)", and "花hua (flower)". We can see clearly that combined characters are associative-compound and pictophonetic. The pictographic elements of the combined characters are shown in their ideographic, or form components; for example "日ri (sun)" and "月yue (moon)" in the associative-compound character "明", and "女nu (female)" in the pictophonetic character "妈". Characters that serve as form components are radicals. According to statistical evidence, among the 2,270 combined characters in 2,500 common Han characters, 70 percent of form components still function to distinguish meaning.

The form component "疒" is a painting of a sickperson lying on a bed.

The Category Meanings of Form Components. Before we can gain a full understanding of form components, we must grasp their category meanings; that is, the basic meaning of a category in terms of its common qualities and features. For example, the form component "氵" represents running water and liquid, and "water" and "liquid" are the category meanings of "氵". Once we understand this, we can learn the combined characters that are related to "water" and "liquid", such as "河 he (river)", "波 bo (wave)", "澡 zao (bath)", "泡 pao (bubble)", "流 liu (flow)", and "油 you (oil)". To take another example, the form component "疒" in ancient characters, represents a sweating person lying on a bed, implying that they are sick. Almost all of the combined Han characters relating to disease have the form component "疒", such as "病 bing (illness)", "疾 ji (disease)", "疗 liao (cure)",

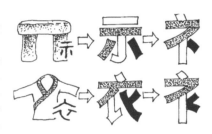

The Origin of the Category Meanings of the Form Components "礻" and "衤"
The form component "礻" originated from a sacrificial alter used in ancient sacrificial ceremonies, and "衤" originated from the upper garment as worn in ancient times.

"疼 teng (pain)", and "痛 tong (ache)". The category meaning of "疒" is "disease". The form components "礻" and "衤" are further examples. In writing, people often misuse the two components, incorrectly writing "神 shen (god)", or "裙 qun (skirt)", because they do not know that "礻" indicates the category meaning of "sacrifice", or that "衤" indicates the category meaning of "cloth." The pictographic elements of the two form components are different.

The components listed in the table below are all form components (independent characters and their variants). Learning the forms and category meanings of the form components is very useful in learning the Han characters.

Category Meanings of Common Form Components					
Form Components	Ancient Character Forms	Category Meanings	Form Components	Ancient Character Forms	Category Meanings
氵		Water and liquid	刂		Knives and using knives
口		Using one's mouth and the manner of speaking	马(馬)		Horses and that which is related to horses
扌		Hands and using hands	𧾷(足)		Feet and using feet
木(木)		Woody plants and wood products	广		Houses
艹		Herbal plants	疒		Disease
亻		Person	页		Head
圡(土)		Land and building	米(米)		Rice and grain
钅		Metal and metal products	酉		Wine and brewing products
纟		Silk and silk products	犭(犬)		Animals
月		Moon and body	衤		Clothes
女(女)		Women	𠂉		Foodstuffs
辶		Walking	礻		Gods and sacrifice
忄		Mentality and emotion	宀(穴)		Caves
日		The sun and time	彳		Walking and roads
火(火)		Fire and high temperatures	灬		Fire
石		Stone	鱼(鱼)		Fish
心		Mentality and emotion	皿		Containers
𥫗(竹)		Bamboo and bamboo products	雨(雨)		Rain
讠		Speaking and language	羽		Feather
贝		Money	衣		Clothing
宀		Houses	彳		Walk
虫		Insects	鸟		Birds
禾(禾)		Seedlings of Cereal crops	冫		Ice and cold
𤣩(王)		Jade and rarity	囗		Encircled
山(山)		Mountain ridges	阝		Earth mountain
目		Eyes	阝		City

Variants of Form Components. In order to make the characters' square forms balanced and aesthetic, the positioning of some form components has altered. For example, when "水 shui (water)" serves as a form component, it is written as "水" in the lower part of the character and as "氵" in the left part of the character. When "心 xin (heart)" serves as the form component, it is written as "忄" in the left part of a character and as "小" in the lower part. It is worth mentioning that many Han characters will change slightly when serving as the left form component. Regarding the variants of form components, "手 shou (hand)" has the most variants and is used the most frequently, examples being "又", "寸" and "攵". Appreciating that they are all variants of "手" is very useful when learning them.

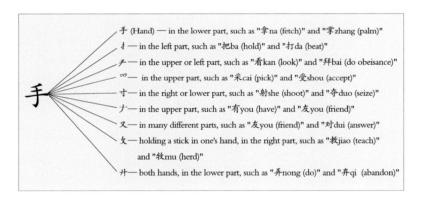

Kaishu	Jiaguwen	Kaishu	Jiaguwen	Kaishu	Jiaguwen	Kaishu	Jiaguwen
立		天		美		化	
步		保		走		网	
初		高		京		宫	

Kaishu (Regular Script)
Jiaguwen (Inscriptions on bones and tortoiseshells from the Shang Dynasty
A comparison between ancient and modern characters.

Form Indicates Meaning

There are many homophones amongst the Han characters. As they cannot be distinguished merely by sound, we can only differentiate their meanings by looking at their forms. Examples are "治病 zhibing (cure disease)" and "致病 zhibing (cause disease)", and "期中考试 qizhongkaoshi (midsemester examination)" and "期终考试 qizhongkaoshi (end-of-term examination)". We can only distinguish the meanings of the homophones by looking at the characters themselves.

战士——战事	因为——音位	雨露——语录
绘画——会话	上级——上集	复数——负数
图画——涂画	世纪——事迹	舒适——书市
经历——精力	独立——独力	销售——消瘦
意义——意译	考察——考查	石油——食油
报酬——报仇	蜜蜂——密封	世界——视界
形式——形势	有利——有力	
权利——权力——全力		
电视——殿试——电示——电势		
事例——势力——势利——视力——示例——市立		

Examples of Homophones
These homophones can only be distinguished by looking at their forms.

辨——辨别	形旁是"刂"(刀)，用刀切开辨别最清楚
辩——辩论	形旁是"讠"(言)，辩论要用语言
辧(办)——办事、办公	办事、办公。形旁是"力"，做事要用力
辫——辫子	形旁是"纟"(丝)，扎辫子要用丝织物

Examples of Characters with Similar Forms
These characters with similar forms must be observed carefully in order to be distinguished.

Mr Zhao Yuanren, a great Chinese philologist, wrote a majestic essay in Chinese using 91 characters, *Shi Shi Shi Shi Shi* (*History of Mr. Shi Eating Lions*). It tells the story of a poet named Shi who ate a Lion. All the characters in the essay are pronounced "shi", and without any corresponding knowledge of the content, we can only hear the sounds "shi shi shi". However, the Han characters, with

*Shi Shi Shi Shi Shi (History of
Mr. Shi Eating Lions)*
"Mr. Shi saw a lion in a market".

施氏食狮史 (赵元任)

石室诗士施氏，嗜狮，誓食十狮。氏时时适市视狮。十时，适十狮适市。是时，适施氏适市。氏视是十狮，恃矢势，使十狮逝世。氏拾是十狮尸，适石室。石室湿，使侍拭石室。石室拭，氏始试食是十狮尸。食时，始识是十狮尸，实十石狮尸。试释是事。

A poet named Shi who lived in a house made of stone liked to eat lion meat and one day swore to eat ten lions. Mr. Shi would often look for lions in the local market. One day, at precisely ten o'clock, ten lions came to the market, closely followed by Mr. Shi. Upon seeing the ten lions he drew his bow and shot them one after the other. Then he dragged their bodies back to his stone house. The house was very humid and he ordered his servants to wipe it down. After his stone house was thoroughly cleaned, Mr. Shi sat down to eat the ten lions. But to his dismay he discovered that each of the ten lions were actually made of stone. Now, please give some thought as to what this story really means.

their varied forms, allow us to read this imaginative and interesting story. In other words, the poem can read, but not heard.

Due to the Han characters' striking visual quality, they allow us to experience art and language at the same time. When we read great works of Chinese literature, we can also appreciate them as works of art.

Chinese literary works display many artistic qualities, giving the reader a sense of aesthetic pleasure. The Han characters, as

Artistic impression of Idioms
The visual imagery of the characters found in idioms such as "同舟共济" and "风雨同舟" enable the reader to understand and appreciate their meaning.

transmitters of these works, can strengthen or deepen the reader's appreciation of them, through the great visual imagery they convey.

"同舟共济" is a common idiom. "舟zhou" is a pictograph of a small boat, and the features of some ancient pictographic characters can still be discerned from it. "同舟tongzhou" means "sitting in the same boat", and "济ji" has the component "three-dot water," which means "crossing a river". "同舟共济" means a group of people crossing water in a boat. The meaning of this idiom is that it takes a joint effort, with people working together, to overcome difficulties. Another Chinese idiom, "风雨同舟" (风feng means wind and 雨yu means rain), has a strong pictograph and a similar meaning to "同舟共济".

These aesthetic lines show bright moonlight filtering through the branches of pine trees, and clear spring water rippling and flowing over pebbles. The ten characters in the picture together create a distinctive and natural visual image, by combining the structures of pictographic, associative-compound, and pictophonetic characters with drawing-like forms.

Artistic Impression of Poems from the Tang Dynasty (618-907)
"明月松间照，清泉石上流 (the bright moon is shining among the pine trees and the clear spring water runs over the pebbles)" - the verses of the *Shan Ju Qiu Ming* (*Dusk in the Mountain Residence in Autumn*) by Wang Wei, a great poet of the Tang Dynasty (618-907 AD).

"Withered vines hanging on old branches
Returning crows croaking at dusk.
A few houses hidden beyond a narrow bridge.
And below the bridge a quiet creek running.
Down a worn path, in the west wind, a
   lean horse comes plodding
The sun dips down in the west
And the lovesick traveler is still at the end of the world"

These are verses from a famous work, *Tian Jing Sha Qui Si* (*Thoughts in Autumn*) by Ma Zhiyuan, a poet from the Yuan Dynasty (1206-1368). The first three verses use pictographic characters to represent nine things, and create a desolate picture. The setting sun conveys the sadness of the traveler. The pictographic characters enhance the artistic nature of the work.

Artistic impression of the *Tian Jing Sha Qiu Si (Thoughts in Autumn)*, a poem from the Yuan Dynasty (1206 - 1368)

Square Han characters are mysterious, their great mystery lying in their pictographic elements and square forms. Pictographic elements play a major role in the learning and use of Han characters. Placing too much emphasis on their pictographic elements is not practical in terms of their modern forms, because they are no longer pictographic. However their pictographic elements are useful in helping us to learn and write them.

Chinese History Narrated in Han Characters

Chinese history not only involves the succession of dynasties, but also tells vivid tales of real life.

What is unique about the Han characters is that many of them represent historical and cultural pictures, and convey images, stories, and the wisdom and philosophy of our ancient ancestors.

Han characters are an interesting means of learning about Chinese history and culture. They can help us understand China's ancient society, and uncover many mysteries.

Social Life in Ancient Times

Just as fossils reveal hidden aspects of the primeval world, the square Han characters also disclose secrets from the past. The earliest formation of Han characters was based on our ancient ancestors' thoughts and understanding as they reflected on the world around them, and also on day-to-day social life at the time. The forms of the ancient Han characters, then, can be viewed as historical and cultural pictures that tell us a great deal about the past. As "living fossils," they may even be more reliable than research carried out by historians.

A Unique Understanding of the World

Stone ware made by primitive people (Paleolithic Age)

The period about 10-40,000 years ago is known as the Neolithic Age, and historians refer to it as the time of "remote antiquity." During this time the human race developed at an extraordinary speed, and laid the foundations of human civilization. Our early ancestors, however, were powerless against the forces of nature, and believed they could only contend with them by using magic. The ancient Han characters illustrate this initial understanding of the world, and provide a unique insight into the beliefs of our earliest Chinese ancestors.

Culture and history developed with the evolution of the earliest human beings. Beginning with Yuanmou Man, Chinese history goes back 1.7 million years, and Chinese civilization is at least 10,000 years old. Did our ancestors recall these remote times when creating the Han characters? What did those memories consist of? The character "xi (former times)" is said to help us answer these important questions.

CHINESE CHARACTERS

【昔】In Jiaguwen "昔xi" is an associative-compound character, composed of "水shui (water)" and "日ri (sun)". It perhaps indicates that time (日) flows like a river (水) and means "the past." Examples of this are the phrases "昔日xiri (in former days)" and "往昔wangxi (in former times)." However, when we research the original meaning of "former days" in detail, and look back at the remote period when the characters were first created, we find that the story is not as simple as it first seems. We might imagine that in our ancestors' memories, a flood would be an event that left the deepest impression. If asked what they meant by "the former days," they may well have answered that it was the time of the flood. In light of this, we can view the pictographic character "昔" as evidence that a great flood took place in remote antiquity.

A Picture of Dayu Regulating Rivers and Watercourses (Stone rubbings of a painting from the Eastern Han Dynasty [25-220 AD])

Noah's Ark - A story from the Bible
Before the flood, God ordered Noah to build an ark in which he, his family, and various animals and plants, would be saved. God then made it rain for 40 days and 40 nights, and everything on the land drowned. The ark came to rest on the top of the mountain of Ararat, and Noah survived.

xī

昔
Kaishu

Jiaguwen

Jinwen

Xiaozhuan

A comparison between the character "人ren (person)" and other characters indicating animals in Jiaguwen "人" stands upright, but animals do not. The characters in this picture are drawn from top to bottom: 人ren (person), 豕(猪)shi (pig), 虎hu (tiger), 马ma (horse), 龙long (dragon), 犬quan (dog), 象xiang (elephant), 兔tu (rabbit), 鼠shu (mouse), 鱼yu (fish), and 龟gui (tortoise).

rén

人

Kaishu

Jiaguwen

Jinwen

Xiaozhuan

【人】 From ape-man to homosapiens, human civilization developed gradually over time. How did the ancient Chinese people view themselves? A clue is in the formation of the character "人ren (person)."

"人" is a pictographic character. In Jiaguwen and Jinwen it shows the profile of a person standing with outstretched arms. The simple strokes show the observational ability of our ancient ancestors, and their understanding of themselves. The ancient form of the character "人" omits all the details of the human body, focusing only on the standing legs and outstretched arms that distinguish us from other animals, and showing that we can walk upright, and use our hands to make and hold tools. This character depicts a standing figure, but the other Jiaguwen figures representing animals, such as "虎hu (tiger)", "马ma (horse)", "龙long (dragon)", "犬quan (dog)", "象xiang (elephant)", "鼠shu (mouse)", and "龟gui (tortoise)", almost all have downward turning tails and legs bending to the left, with the exception of "鹿lu (deer)", "牛niu (ox)", and "羊yang (sheep)". This suggests that the ancient people differentiated themselves from animals through the characters' forms, and understood themselves to have a prominent position in the scheme of nature. This is reflected in the common saying, "man is the soul of all things." In ancient times, heaven, earth and man were referred to as the "three talents," with heaven above, earth below, and man in between. This not only indicated that "man is the soul of all things," but also showed that ancient people blended man into nature, and essentially identified themselves with the natural world. This reflects the ancient philosophy of "the combination of heaven and man."

" 人 " has the simplest form, being composed of just two strokes, a left-falling and a right-falling stroke. In modern China there is a song that contains the lyric, "the structure of the character ' 人 ' indicates mutual support." This character not only displays a mutually-supportive structure through its left- and right-falling strokes; it also illustrates how Chinese people attach great significance to their interpersonal relationships, and that help, support, unity and harmony, are very important to them.

【天】 The sky is high above us, and is thought to be remote, strong, and mysterious. Because the ancient people regarded it with reverence, the character " 天 tian (sky)" was created with " 人 " as its coordinate.

In Jiaguwen the character " 天 tian (heaven)" looks like a person standing and facing the reader The person's head is given specific prominence, so the original meaning of " 天 " was "top of head" and also indicated the sky. Because the sky is has no boundaries, the ancient people called it " 苍 天 cangtian (boundless sky)." " 天 " also generally refers to the cycle of nature, and many natural things incorporate the character " 天 ", such as " 天文 tianwen (astronomy)", " 天气 tianqi (weather)", " 天 然 tianran (natural)", " 春天 chuntian (spring)", " 秋天 qiutian (autumn)", " 今天 jintian (today)", and " 明天

"Beijing Man," some 500,000 years ago People were able to stand up, make and use tools with their hands, and bake food on a fire.

tiān

Kaishu

Jiaguwen

Jinwen

Xiaozhuan

mingtian (tomorrow)." The sky is where we see the sun, moon, and stars, and is also the source of wind, rain, and thunderstorms. Because ancient people did not understand these natural phenomena, they thought the sky was a magical and supreme god, so they called it "天神tianshen (sky god)", "天帝tiandi (sky god)", and "上天shangtian (heaven)." There was a saying in ancient China that "the sky is round and the earth is square." At the Temple of Heaven in Beijing, the emperors of the Ming (1368-1644) and Qing (1644-1911) Dynasties made sacrifices to heaven. The buildings all had a rounded shape, and blue roofs that symbolized the sky. In order to enhance their prestige, the emperors used "天" to refer to themselves, giving themselves the name "天子tianzi (sons of the heavens)."

The sacred sky, however, was not without its troubles. In ancient China there was a popular tale *Nu Wa Bu Tian* (*Nu Wa Mended the Sky*). The story says that in remote antiquity there was a big hole in the sky, which caused the world disorder, floods, fires, and ferocious animals, making life impossible for the

The Temple of Heaven in Beijing

people. Later a grand goddess named Nu Wa, with a woman's head and a snake's body, fired five-colour stones into the sky, which fixed the hole, and restored peace to the world. This story reflected the ancient people's fear of the sky and showed their strong desire to conquer and change the natural world. This ancient Chinese understanding of nature is strikingly similar to today's situation with the ozone layer and global warming.

Picture of Nu Wa Mending the Sky

【地】 In comparison to "天tian (sky)", "地di (earth)" has a closer relationship with human beings. Our feet are anchored to the earth, and the things we use and eat all belong to the earth. The character "地" looks like a mother giving birth. This is the basis of the character "地", which conveys these concepts.

"地" is an associative-compound character. The left component is "土tu (dust)", and the right component is "也ye (also)." In terms of the characters' origin, "也" represents the female (according to the *Shuowen Jiezi* by Xu Shen, it refers to the private parts of a woman). When "也" is combined with "土"to form the character "地", dust is likened to a mother from which everything originates. This is also reflected in the well-known phrase "大地母亲dadimuqin (mother earth)."

"地" opposes "天", because the sky is above and the earth is below, and the ancient people believed that the two came into being at the same time. In ancient China there was a popular myth, *Pan Gu Kai Tian Pi Di* (*The Creation of the Sky and the Earth by Pan Gu*). It says that long ago, the universe was in chaos, and one day a man named Pan Gu raised his huge axe to "cleave" the chaos. With a huge crash, the chaos was broken, and the things that were light and clear rose up to form the sky, and the things that were heavy and dirty descended to form the earth. After that the sky rose up every day, and the earth deepened every day, and Pan Gu, who stood between

dì

地

Kaishu

坤

Xiaozhuan

"自强不息 Ziqiangbuxi (Constantly Strive to Become Stronger)" and "厚德载物 Houdezaiwu (Carry things with Generous Virtue)": Ancient people had much respect for the sky and the earth. The ancient book *Zhou Yi* strongly praised them with the phrase "天行健，君子以自强不息；地势坤，君子以厚德载物". Its meaning refers to two natural things, the sky and the earth, and says that they have outstanding virtues; the sky extends infinitely and endures forever, and the earth is enormous and gentle, and carries all things on its broad shoulders. It was said that men of honor should also possess such qualities. "自强不息" is one of the basic characteristics of Chinese national identity.

the two, became taller and taller with every sunrise. He was afraid that the earth and sky would join back together, so he stood with his feet on the earth for 18,000 years, using his hands to hold up the sky. By this time sky had become very high and the earth very deep, and Pan Gu, exhausted, collapsed to the ground and died – and that was how the earth and sky came into being.

Ancient Chinese people worshipped the sky and earth. The ancient emperors would hold sacrificial ceremonies for the sky and the earth on Taishan Mountain, and the emperors of the Ming and Qing Dynasties held sacrificial ceremonies to the sky and earth at the Temple of Heaven and Temple of Earth in Beijing. On their wedding day, couples bow to heaven and earth, and the word for this, "拜天地 baitiandi," has become another word for wedding in China. There are many idioms related to both "天" and "地",

The Taishan Mountain, in the Eastern High Mountains (东岳): In ancient times there was a saying that referred to the "five high mountains (五岳)", i.e. the Taishan Mountain in the east(Dong东), the Huashan Mountain in the west, the Hengshan Mountain in the north, the Hengshang Mountain in the south, and the Songshan Mountain in the center. "岳 yue" means "high mountain." From the time of Emperor Qinshihuang of the Qin Dynasty (221-206 BC), many emperors would climb the Taishan Mountain to hold sacrificial ceremonies to the heaven and the earth. These rituals were known as "封禅 fēngshàn."

such as "天长地久tianchangdijiu (everlasting)," "天南地北tiannandibei (far apart)," "天高地厚tiangaodihou (immensity of the universe)," "天时地利tianshidili (favorable climate and geographic conditions)," "天经地义tianjingdiyi (unalterable principles)," "天罗地网tianluodiwang (tight encirclement)," "天翻地覆tianfandifu (state of extreme confusion, represented by the inversion of the sky and the earth)," "天崩地裂tianbengdilie (breaking of the sky and the earth)," and "天圆地方tianyuandifang (the sky is round and the earth is square)." These are all well-known Chinese idioms.

Picture of Pan Gu Creating the Sky and the Earth

【神】 In primitive society, the powers of nature were a constant threat, and people believed that natural things had supernatural powers. When the ancient Chinese people first began to write, they were living in constant fear of nature, and represented supernatural forces in characters, such as "神shen (god)" and "鬼gui (ghost)". The formation of the character "神" is the most illustrative of this.

In the minds of our ancient ancestors, the gods were omnipresent supernatural spirits, who ruled the earth and sky. In Jiaguwen there is a character that looks like an "S"-shaped curve, connecting the two. The upper part resembles a huge, mysterious hand reaching out to the sky and earth. This is the character "申shen," the original form of the character "神". On careful observation, we can see that the "S"-shaped curve looks like lightning during a thunderstorm. Lightening was also considered back then to be mysterious and supernatural, so "神" probably originated from people's fear of it. Many philologists think "申" is the original character of "电".

In fairy tales and religious writing, gods are the creators and masters of everything in the world. They have infinite supernatural powers, and people regard them with awe. The ancient Chinese people believed in many gods, such as the God of Heaven, the God of

shén

神

Kaishu

Jiaguwen

Jinwen

Xiaozhuan

Earth, the Grain God, Pan Gu, Nu Wa, the God of the Sun, Yuhuang Dadi (the Jade Empeoror), Wang Mu Niang Niang (the Queen Mother of the West), the God of the Kitchen, and the Square God - all important Gods in ancient times. Many people believed that their souls would live on after their deaths, and these invisible souls were also regarded as gods.

Pious Totem Worship

Totem worship was a common ritual in remote antiquity. Many primitive cultures around the world worshipped natural phenomena like the sun and moon, and mountains, rivers, and animals. In the early characters, Chinese people directly adopted the totem signs of their clans, and these have left a reliable testimony of primitive totem worship.

Formation of the Character "神shen (God)"
Two large and mysterious hands extending towards heaven and earth.

lóng

龙

Kaishu

Jiaguwen

Jinwen

龍

Xiaozhuan

【龙】"龙long (dragon)" is the biggest totem in China, earning it the title of the "No. 1 Totem in China."

The character "龙" in Jiaguwen and Jinwen has many forms. It usually has a thin body, horns on its head, and an open mouth, so it really does resemble a dragon. In Xiaozhuan, however, we can no longer see the shape of a dragon, and in Kaishu, the complex form of "龙(龍)" seems to have become totally abstract. If we analyse the character's form, however, we can still find the image of a dragon. The left part is the dragon's head, while "立" is its horns, "月" is its mouth, and the right part is its body. The Chinese dragon has a very unusual shape. It exists only in people's imagination, and archaeologists believe that it was a totemic integration, inspired mainly by the snake. It has the body of a snake, the head of a pig, the horns of a deer, the ears of an ox, the beard of a goat, the scales of a fish, and the claws of an eagle. We

The "Nine-Dragon Wall" in the Imperial Palace in Beijing
These nine dragons were imperial dragons with five claws, and ordinary people could not use them in decoration.

cannot see all of these features in the ancient character, but the basic shapes of a large head and a long body are very clear.

The image of the Chinese dragon reveals an historical fact. In remote antiquity the Huazia Clan in the Yellow River Valley used the snake as its totem, and under the leadership of the Yellow Emperor, the clan conquered and formed alliances with other clans to form a large united tribe. The Huaxia Clan's principle totem – the snake – was combined with the totems of other clans – pig, deer, ox, sheep, fish and eagle – to form a composite totem of the Huaxia Clan, which was the dragon totem. The allied community of the Huaxia Clan later became the Chinese nation. Archaeologists have unearthed a dragon made of shells from an ancient tomb in Henan Province. At some 6,000 years old, it is the oldest dragon in China, and is known as the "No. 1 Dragon in China." A number of beautiful jade dragons have also been discovered among the ruins of the Hongshan Culture, which flourished 5,000 years ago. These imply that the dragon was predominant in remote antiquity.

Unlike the Western dragon, which breathes fire, the Chinese dragon spat water from its mouth, which was thought to have caused wind and rain. China is an agricultural country, so its people

A Large Jade Pig-headed Dragon from 5,000 Years Ago (the Time of the Hongshan Culture)
This was the totem of the Hongshan people, and has become the representative symbol of the Hongshan Culture.

fèng

凤

Kaishu

Jiaguwen

Jinwen

Xiaozhuan

have always hoped for weather that will yield a good harvest. In ancient times there were temples dedicated to the dragon king all over China, and people would go to them in times of draught, to pray to him for rain. The dragon symbol, then, was a direct result of Chinese agricultural civilization. The dragon was the most important totem in ancient China. After the Han Dynasty (206 BC – 220 AD), emperors successively adopted it for 2,000 years. These emperors referred to themselves as the "sons of the real dragon." The Imperial Palace in Beijing – a residence of past emperors - contains many carvings and drawings of dragons. The Taihe Palace (the largest Imperial Palace), for example, contains 12,654 dragon drawings, earning it the nickname "a world of dragons."

【凤】 Like "龙long (dragon)," "凤fèng (phoenix)" is also an ancient totem. According to the theory of Yin (feminine) and Yang (masculine), the dragon is Yang and the phoenix Yin, so people often associate the two. Examples are "龙飞凤舞longfeifengwu (being lively and vigorous like a flying dragon and a dancing phoenix)" and "龙凤呈祥longfengchengxiang (dragon and phoenix indicate luck)." The Chinese people consider the phoenix to bring good luck, and many years ago the character "凤" also appeared frequently in paintings. In fairy tales, the phoenix is a lucky and sacred bird with beautiful bright feathers, wearing a princess's coronet on its head. It has a long tail and looks similar to a peacock.

In Jiaguwen, the character "凤" depicts a bird, and its coronet and extended tail are clearly represented. The character "凤 (𩾔)" is definitely pictographic. Jiaguwen also has another character, "凤 (𩾌)." It has a pictophonetic component, "凡", which indicates sound alongside the form of "凤". It follows the form of "鸟niao (bird)" and the sound of "凡fan." "凤" is commonly known as "凤凰", but specialists are certain that "凤" is male and "凰" is female. It

In a traditional Chinese wedding, the bride wears phoenix coronet, and a robe embroidered with phoenix patterns.

was believed that "凤" was the king of all birds, and that when it flew into the sky, ten thousand other birds would follow it. It was also believed that with the appearance of "凤", the world would enter a time of peace and security. The bird "凤" was thought to bring good luck, so it was worshipped and became a totem.

Like the dragon, the phoenix is an imaginary animal, and represented the most advanced development in bird totems. The oldest phoenix drawing in China was excavated in Hunan Province in 2004. It consisted of two phoenixes, both with an elegant, peacock-like posture, carved onto a white clay plot. Specialists believe that phoenix worship in China goes back 7,400 years, so it is a truly ancient Chinese tradition. According to textual research, phoenix worship in remote antiquity was a type of bird worship. At that time, the Dongyi people in the East used a bird as their totem, as did the people of the famous Shang Dynasty. This is shown in the verses from *Shi Jing* (*Classics of Poetry*); for example "天命玄鸟, 降而生商 (God's dark bird descended on the earth and gave birth to the Shang Dynasty). This dark bird referred to here is a phoenix, which was the totem

Phoenix Coronet unearthed from Ding Mausoleum, in the Ming Dynasty (1368 - 1644)

of the ancestors of the Shang Dynasty. The Shang Dynasty is believed to have come about because of the phoenix.

Eternal Ancestor Worship

Chinese people began to worship their ancestors in the days of the ancient patriarchal clan communities. They believed that their ancestors gave them life, and that their souls could protect their children, so they would worship and make sacrifices to them. Because ancestors are the basis for the continuation of both clans and individuals, they have been worshipped for thousands of years. This has continued to the present day, and has outlived the worship of divinities.

【祖】 Knowing the meaning of "祖zu (ancestor)," helps us to understand the essence of ancestor worship. Ancestors are the basis for the continuation of both clans and individuals.

zǔ

Kaishu

Jiaguwen

Jinwen

Xiaozhuan

In Jiaguwen the character was written as "且" and in Jinwen a component "礻" was added. "祖" means ancestor - the elder generation of a clan or family, and those in their family's or community's remote past. The Yellow and Yan Emperors, for example, were known as "The ancestors of the Chinese nation." According to the *Shuowen Jiezi*, "祖, 始庙也 ('祖' is the temple were sacrificial ceremonies for ancestors are held)," makes a clear reference to ancestors. The "礻" in the character indicates worship and sacrifice, and the "且" component illustrates the memorial tablet used for sacrificing ancestor's souls. It serves as a symbol of those ancestors, and is a pictographic character of "土tu (clay), from which everything was thought to have been initially created. It could illustrate the fact that ancestors have tens of thousands of descendents, or it could represent genitalia, by means of which children are conceived. In remote antiquity the phallic worship shown in

Sacrifice to the Mausoleum of the Yellow Emperor. The Yellow Emperor is seen as the ancestor of the Chinese nation. The mausoleum of the Yellow Emperor in Shaanxi is the place where Chinese people pay their respects to him. A grand sacrificial ceremony would be held there during the annual Qingming Festival.

the character "祖" was very widespread, and it appears on many surviving pottery, stone, and wooden objects from the time. The old saying, "ancestors are the root of the continuation of clans and their individual members," captures the essence of ancestor worship. Just like "宗zong (ancestral temple)," the formation of character "祖" not only expresses the ancient Chinese people's respect for, and worship of, their ancestors, but it also reflects their worship of nature and genitalia.

Chinese people still highly respect their ancestors. They are usually named after their fathers, and call their father's father "祖父zufu (grandfather)" and their mother's father "外祖父waizufu (maternal grandfather)". These customs can all be traced back to primitive patriarchal clan society. For some Chinese people, remembering their ancestors is an important part of their lives. This is known as "光宗耀祖guangzongyaozu (bringing honor to one's ancestors)."

Revealing Ancient Civilization

Photos and pictures can provide authentic records of things. Just like pictures, Han characters record the evolution of ancient civilization, and are very clear and interesting. Characters are one of the most effective means of learning about history and culture. Through their drawing-like nature, and by indicating meaning through form, they reveal a significant amount about the development of ancient civilization in China, and are viewed as a wonder of the world.

The Evolution of Ancient Substantial Civilization

In remote antiquity, Chinese society underwent several stages of development, progressing from fishing and hunting to the raising of livestock, and from gathering to agriculture. The ancient Han characters, just like pictures and photographs, provide lasting records of these various stages of development.

Pottery basin painted with fish with men's heads (from the Yangshao Culture, unearthed from the Banpo Ruins)
A Fish with a Man's Head, painted onto pottery, was the totem of the Banpo Clan and has become a symbol of the Banpo Culture.

Fishing and hunting were important pursuits in early human history. We can learn a lot from rock paintings in China and mural cave paintings in Europe, left behind at the end of primitive society; however Han characters tell us even more.

【渔】 "鱼 yu (fish)" is a noun. This ancient character is pictographic, showing the head, body, and tail of a fish. It specifically represents a fish that has just been caught. "渔 yu (fish)" is the verb "to fish,"

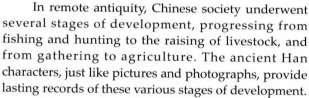

yú

渔

Kaishu

Jiaguwen

Jiaguwen

Jiaguwen

relating to the activity of fishing. Many earthenware items excavated from the Banpo ruins in Xi'an, where people lived 6,000 years ago, have paintings of fish on them, and various fishing tools have also been discovered, such as nets and hooks, which indicate that fishing was an important activity at the time. In Xiaotun Village, Anyang, Henan Province, where lots of Jiaguwen pieces were unearthed, many fish bones were also excavated, including those of cyprinoid, grass carp, and mackerel. These fish were all commonly used as food. Jiaguwen also has some characters related to fishing, such as "渔" and "网wang (net)." This indicates that in the Shang Dynasty, fishing developed further. Among these characters, "渔" originally meant "fishing," but is now a pictographic character with the elements "水shui (water)" and "鱼 yu (fish)." In Jiaguwen it is an associative-compound character with many forms. In the picture, the four Jiaguwen characters of "渔" reflect at least three kinds of fishing that were carried out at the time; fishing by hand, fishing with a hook and line, and fishing with a net. The fourth form was "渔", which is still in use today. Appreciating the Jiaguwen characters of "渔" not only tells us about the fishing methods of past times, but also gives us important historical

Character "鱼yu (fish)" in Jinwen
This is a pictographic character in the shape of a fish. On close observation we can see that it represents many fish tied together, so the form of the ancient character "鱼" give us a sense of ancient fishing and hunting.

Picture of fishing from the Shang Dynasty
In Jiaguwen the character "渔yu (to fish)", showed several of the fishing methods employed 3,000 years ago.

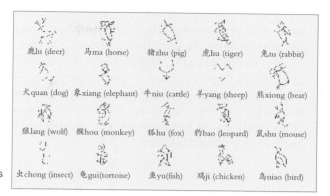

Examples of animal characters in Jiaguwen

鹿lu (deer)	马ma (horse)	猪zhu (pig)	虎hu (tiger)	兔tu (rabbit)
犬quan (dog)	象xiang (elephant)	牛niu (cattle)	羊yang (sheep)	熊xiong (bear)
狼lang (wolf)	猴hou (monkey)	狐hu (fox)	豹bao (leopard)	鼠shu (mouse)
虫chong (insect)	龟gui(tortoise)	鱼yu(fish)	鸡ji (chicken)	鸟niao (bird)

information. During and before the Shang Dynasty, fishing had become one of the most important daily means of food, and had become a relatively advanced pursuit.

There are many characters that describe our ancient ancestors' hunting activities, and they are all strikingly clear. We will now look at some of these.

zhú

Kaishu

Jiaguwen

Jinwen

Xiaozhuan

【逐】In Jiaguwen the character "逐zhu (chase)" is an associative-compound character and originally meant "chase." The upper part of the character represents a pig (豕shi) and the lower part represents a person's feet (止). The form of this character clearly illustrates a wild boar being chased by a hunter, and represents the hunting and killing of animals. Jiaguwen has a character "射she (shoot)," which shows a hand drawing a bow. The bow would have been aimed at a wild animal. In Jiaguwen there are many characters that represent hunting. For example, "网wang (net)" indicates fishing and hunting, "敢gan (bold)" shows a hand holding a three-pronged spear (which later evolved to a trap for capturing wild boars), "坠(墜 zhuì) fall" shows the act of chasing and trapping a wild boar, "罗(羅)luo (catching birds with a net)" depicts the use of a net to catch birds, and

"获(獲)huo (capture)" shows the capture of a bird by hand. The actual animals hunted by the early people can also be found in Jiaguwen, such as "鹿lu (deer)", "野牛yeniu (wild ox)", "野猪yezhu (wild boar)", "兔tu (rabbit)", "马ma (horse)", "虎hu (tiger)", "熊xiong (bear)", "鱼yu (fish)", and "鸟niao (bird)." Jiaguwen had many characters depicting animals, revealing the close relationship between ancient people and the animals they hunted and ate.

Shooting wild animals

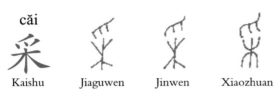

cǎi			
采			
Kaishu	Jiaguwen	Jinwen	Xiaozhuan

【采】 Gathering was the first stage in the evolution of agriculture, and the character "采cai (collection)" illustrates this activity.

Before the emergence of agriculture, wild plants were the most important source of food, and the pursuit of gathering them had flourished. According to the ancient Chinese fairy tale *Shen Nong Tasted Hundreds of Herbs*, the gatherer Shen Nong discovered 72 poisonous varieties in one day. This anecdote tells us how important the gathering of wild plants was in early civilization. Accounts of it are also recorded in *Shi Jing (Classics of Poetry)*. In the *Shuowen Jiezi* there were 1,097 Han characters relating to plants. Shen Nong must have tasted many more herbs than the 72 he was allegedly poisoned by, and his brave pursuits showed people which plants were edible and which were not, thus they could avoid getting sick from things they ate. This collection activity was recorded most directly in the Han character "采" It is an associative-compound character, which appeared in Jiaguwen with the upper part depicting a hand, and the lower part depicting a tree bearing fruit. Together

Ancient rock painting showing the chasing and shooting of yaks in Qinghai
This was a painting by Chinese people 10,000 years ago, and is an authentic illustration of the hunting of wild yaks at that time.

Picture of people collecting mulberry leaves (Pattern on Bronze Ware from the Warring States Period (475-221BC))

Shen Nong Tasted Hundreds of Herbs: Shen Nong, also known as the Yandi Emperor, is the god of the sun in ancient Chinese folklore. He was said to have had an ox's head and snake's body. He taught people how to make farming implements, drilled wells for water, planted five kinds of grain, and was the representative figure of the gathering and farming phase in China's history. The story that he tasted hundreds of herbs is very well known. It says that at the dawn of the farming period, people were still eating wild herbs, fruit and small insects, and drinking unboiled water, so they would often get ill. Despite the dangers to himself, Shen Nong tasted hundreds of herbs and spring waters, and told people what could be eaten and what could not. He also discovered a range of agricultural crops, teas, and herbal medicines, and it is said that he once encountered 72 kinds of poisonous plants in a single day. He finally died from eating poisonous grass, and he continues to be highly respected by the Chinese people today.

the two components mean "picking." In Jinwen the fruit on the tree is omitted, and the character in Kaishu style evolved from Xiaozhuan.

【农】 In ancient China, agriculture advanced very early. The country was founded on agriculture as a national policy, and the Chinese have always placed great importance on food as a means of survival. Ancient China was very agricultural, and even now farmers still form the majority of the country's population. It is, however, difficult to deduce the meaning of the character "nong (agriculture)." As a major agricultural country, China is not only abundant with crops, but also has a renowned tradition of intensive cultivation. This tradition lies in the farmers' use of agricultural implements, their methods for planting and cultivating crops, and their field management. These are all fully represented in the ancient Han characters. For example "田tian (field)" looks like a field, "耒lei (plough)" and "耜si (ploughshares)" look like farming implements that are used to plough the soil, "利li (sharp)" indicates the shearing of grain, "犁li (plough)" illustrates a plough being pulled by an ox, "耕geng (furrow)" indicates the furrowing of soil with a hand-plough, "协xie (joint)" shows three people together ploughing a field together, and "留liu (stay)" indicates the irrigation of fields. The character "艺yi (skill)" shows a pair of hands planting seeds, and reveals that the ancient people viewed this as a particular skill. "农" originally

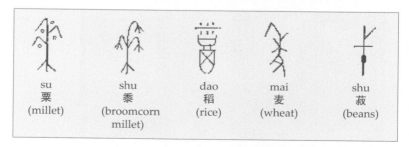

| su
粟
(millet) | shu
黍
(broomcorn millet) | dao
稻
(rice) | mai
麦
(wheat) | shu
菽
(beans) |

"五谷wugu (five grains)" in Ancient Characters

117

meant hoeing weeds or harvesting. In Jiaguwen, the character's upper part consists of "草cao (grass)" and "木mu (tree)" indicating grains, and the lower part is "辰(chén)", a pictograph of somebody holding a stone harrow with both hands. In Jinwen "田tian (field)" was added between "草" and "木", which clarified the meaning: farmers hoed weeds and harvested fields with stone harrows. After the change to Lishu, the upper part was combined into "曲", and the character was written as "農" (the complex form of the character "农"). Back in the days of remote antiquity, people hoed and harvested using a stone shaft, so it is obvious that this character appeared very early, and that people were engaged in agricultural activity from very early times.

For hundreds, even thousands of years, successive generations of Chinese people have farmed and harvested in fields. They start work at sunrise, dig wells for drinking water, and farm to produce food. They are self-sufficient, and rarely leave their land and their hometowns. These simple, honest farmers care deeply about the harvest season and all aspects of farming, but they pay little attention to things beyond their experience, such as the afterlife. They wish only for good weather, sufficient food and clothing, and peaceful lives. This ethos has been attributed to

nóng

Kaishu

Jiaguwen

Jinwen

Xiaozhuan

Farmers Working in Fields in a Traditional Way

田 tian (field): in the form of a pane-shaped sown field

井 jing (well): the form of a water well with a square mouth

耒 lei (plough): a tool to plough with tynes at its end

耜 si (spade-like plough): a spade-like plough

力 li: sharp-headed ploughing implement

刀 dao (knife): a tool to cut logs

斤 jin: axe-shaped tool to cut wood

耕 geng: ploughing a field with the plough in both hands

疆 jiang: measure fields by means of a bow

苗 miao: seedlings are growing in the fields

焚 fen (burn): start a fire to reduce the grass on waste land to stubble

楚 chu: enter the forest to fell trees

艺 yi: a person is planting seedling with both hands

协 xie: three persons sowing together

封 feng: plant a seedling with both hands

秉 bing: hold a seedling in one's hand

秦 qin: take hold of a pestle and pound rice

利 li: harvest crops with a scythe

奉 feng: hold tree seedlings in one's hands

留 liu: dig out channels to irrigate fields

Examples of Jiaguwen Describing Farming Activities

the Chinese as part of their "national character." Their tendency to emphasize reality and personal experience has had a profound influence on the development of Chinese culture.

【年】 "年 nian (year)" is not only a noun indicating time; it is also a symbol of China's agricultural culture.

"年" is a character highly regarded by the Chinese people, and they call their Spring Festival (Chinese New Year) "过年

guonian". "年" has a direct relationship with agriculture. In Jiaguwen and Jinwen, the character's upper part is "禾he (standing grain)" and the lower part is "人ren (person)." The whole form looks like a person carrying a sheaf of grain on their back, which indicates harvest. In the Shuowen Jiezi, "年" was defined as "grain becomes ripe"; in other words "harvest", and called "受年shounian". At that time, grain ripened once a year, so its meaning was extended to "岁sui (year)." One "年" is one "岁". This indicates that during the Shang and Zhou Dynasties, China was already an agricultural society. "过年guonian" originates from "腊祭laji" in the Shang Dynasty, 3,000 years ago.

"腊la" was a type of sacrifice in ancient times. Laborers would work hard in the fields to reap the harvest, and then, in "腊月" (layue), the twelfth lunar month of the year, they would hold sacrificial rituals to the gods, heaven, the earth, and their ancestors. The Spring Festival is the oldest and grandest traditional Chinese folk festival, and demonstrates their distinctive agricultural pursuits. Experiencing a Spring Festival in China gives us a real understanding of the thoughts, emotions and customs of the Chinese people. In the Temple of Heaven in Beijing, the emperors of the Ming and Qing Dynasties held sacrificial ceremonies to heaven. This was partly because they wanted to show that "their sovereignty was granted by the gods" - because they believed that the gods had ordered them to serve as emperors – but it was also so that they could pray for good weather and a fruitful harvest. The largest building in the Temple of Heaven is "Qinian (祈年) Palace." "祈年" menas "祈谷 (grain)", so the palace is named after its use, for praying to the gods for a good harvest.

nián

Kaishu

Jiaguwen

Jinwen

Xiaozhuan

Marriage and Family

Marriage and having a family is one of the most important aspects of Chinese civilization. The forms of the ancient characters tell us a lot about this.

"过年guonian (spend the Spring Festival)" originated from the Sacrifice in the Last Lunar Month (腊祭laji), in the Shang Dynasty

ān

Kaishu

Jiaguwen

Jinwen

Xiaozhuan

【安】 "安an (stability)" is a character with a high cultural value, representing the era of marriage within communities, and a maternal society. It is an associative compound character, and in Jiaguwen, its outer part depicts the form of a house, and its inner part a kneeling woman. The image of a women kneeling in a house represents stability and placidity, which was the original meaning of the character "安". A woman in a house implied that she was married with a family, and so was leading a stable life. However this character tells us even more in cultural terms. "安" is an old character, and its formation reflects the ancient condition on marriage that "only mothers were known and fathers were unknown." In the later period of this society, people no longer had to marry within their clan, and a woman could find a spouse outside of her clan (spouse marriage). If she did so, she would have to leave her childhood home. A woman who owned a house and had her own family was assumed to feel content, thus women were believed to make clans more stable.

【娶】 "娶qu (marry a wife)" is a character that depicts marriage in a patriarchal society.

The character that indicates a man getting married and taking a girl into his family, is "娶qu", as

121

in "娶亲quqin (get married)", "娶妻quqi (take a wife)", "娶媳妇quxifu (take a wife)", and "娶老婆qulaopo (take a wife)." In Jiaguwen it is written as "取qu (take)", and according to the *Shuowen Jiezi*, "娶(qu) means "取妇(take a woman)". Therefore it seems that the first character "取" was used to indicate marriage. "取(𠂤)" is an associative-compound character. The left part is "耳er (ear)" and the right part is "手shou (hand)", which together illustrate a hand holding an ear. Its original meaning was "obtaining by force." In ancient battles, when people took captives or killed enemies, they would cut off their victim's left ear as a trophy. Because this character was also used for marriage, it implied that marriage was considered at the time to be the taking of a woman by force. Later the form component "女nu (female)" was added to the character "取", and the pictophonetic character "娶" was created. This took away the connotation of marrying a woman against her will, and gave it a more positive interpretation.

Formation of the Character "安 an (safety)"
An adult woman quietly kneeling in her house, and feeling calm and peaceful. The corresponding character is said to evoke a similar feeling in the reader.

【家】 The form of the character "家jia (house)" is unusual, but nonetheless a true reflection on how things were in ancient times, in terms of the emergence of

qǔ

Kaishu

Jiaguwen

Xiaozhuan

Formation of the Character "婚hun (marriage)"
The act of seizing a woman by force after dark

A happy Chinese wedding today

ancient houses, and people's knowledge of how to build a home.

"家" is also an old character. In respect of form, it is an associative-compound character, with "豕(猪) (pig)" underneath "宀", depicting a pig inside a house. What did this mean? Back in the days when people had just started to establish settled homes and families, hunting and agriculture became more sophisticated, resulting in an abundance of game and grain, and people began to raise animals. They raised pigs, cattle, sheep, dogs, chicken, and horses, which were collectively referred to as the "six livestock" by the ancient people. Pigs were the most important of the six, as they were both a major food source and a symbol of wealth and social status. We can see in Chinese museums that pig bones were buried with the heads of ancient clans, and people of high social standing might have had dozens of pigs buried alongside them. Archaeologists have discovered many houses in the ruins of remote antiquity, where people lived in the upper part, and pigs were raised in the lower part. The character "家" – showing a place where people both lived and kept pigs - represented this type of combined dwelling for people and livestock.

jiā

Kaishu

Jiaguwen

Jinwen

Xiaozhuan

【好】 After marrying and settling down, people would consider having a family, a concept that seems to have emerged very early in Chinese culture.

The character "好hao (good)" reflects the survival instinct of the ancient Chinese ancestors, and is both simple and profound. It also means very.

"好" is an associative-compound character and is composed of "女nu (female)" and "子zi (baby)", depicting a woman giving birth. The ancient Chinese people believed that children would strengthen a clan and continue its bloodline, so their birth was considered the best thing that could happen, and the woman who had the most babies, was held in the highest esteem. This attitude reflected the ancestors' strong survival instinct. It was important in ancient China to have lots of children, and each family hoped to have four living generations at any one time. There were believed to be "three kinds of disobedience," not having children being the most serious. Therefore having children was very important to a woman, and women were judged on how fertile they were. A large number of laborers were needed for agriculture, and families wanted to continue their bloodline, so children were very important for both. The situation is very different today.

In modern Chinese, "好" has many meanings, such as "excellent," "friendly," "close," "easy," "completely," and "especially." It can also be pronounced "hao," and used as a verb, meaning "to love" and "to like"; for example "我好唱歌,她好跳舞 I like singing and she likes dancing." Learners of Chinese will be familiar with this phenomenon.

【孝】 "孝xiao (filial piety; respect for elders)" was one of the most advocated moral standards in ancient feudal society. Respecting and serving one's parents is known as "孝", or "孝顺xiaoshun (filial piety)". "孝" is an interesting associative-compound

Formation of the Character "家jia (house)" A Pig in a House.

Formation of the Character "好 hao (good)" Women who produce babies are "好 (good)"

hǎo

好   𢀸   𢀸   𡥉

Kaishu   Jiaguwen   Jinwen   Xiaozhuan

xiào

Kaishu

Jiaguwen

Jinwen

Xiaozhuan

character. In Jiaguwen, the lower part of the character is "子zi (baby)" and the upper part resembles grass. Its meaning is not quite clear; it might have meant that children wore flowers and grass on their heads and played games to entertain their elders. In Jinwen, however, the meaning of the character"孝" is much clearer. The upper part of the character depicts an old man with a hunchback and very little hair, and the lower part depicts a child being supported by him, or carried on his back. This illustrated an act of respect towards one's elders, demonstrating filial piety, and was the original meaning of the character. Confucius advocated "孝" and regarded it as the most important aspect of family life. His statement "弟子入则孝", said that children should respect and obey their parents and grandparents, no matter what they said or did. This wasn't necessarily right, but even today, showing respect for the generations above is a seen as virtuous and is an important moral standard. Those who do not adhere to this are not highly respected in China.

The Cruelty of War

"战争zhanzheng (war)" is a terrible tragedy, but one that has happened all too often in the course of world history. China's history has witnessed countless wars between clans, between ruling groups, between people and rulers, and between farmers and nomads. The Han characters recorded the history of war, and some vividly illustrated its inherent violence.

Formation of the Character "孝xiao (filial piety)"
A child helping an elder along a walkway.

【戈】"戈gē (battle-axe)" was a commonly used weapon, so it became a symbol of weaponry and war. Many characters related to these two things include the form of "戈".

"戈" was a common weapon during the Shang and Zhou Dynasties, 3,000 years ago. The character "戈" is a pictographic character. In Jiaguwen it clearly displays the form of the battle-axe. It shows a long pole, and the extended cross line above it is the blade. In Jinwen, the character became even more specific. The blade surmounting the shaft looks more like a dagger, and at the base of the pole there is a fork that can be inserted into the ground. "戈" appeared very early, and archaeologists have discovered many stone "戈" in ruins from the later part of the Neolithic age. These might also represent the axes that were used back then to fell trees. During the Shang and Zhou Dynasties, the Spring and Autumn Period (110-475 BC), and the Warring States Period (475-221 BC), the head of a "戈" was usually made of bronze, and there were two kinds, short-pole and long-pole "戈". Infantrymen used the short-pole "戈" in hand-to-hand fighting, and charioteers used the long-pole "戈", the length of which could be as much as three meters. In the Western Han Dynasty (206 BC-25 AD), due to a rise in the popularity of iron ware, "戈" gradually disappeared from the battlefields and another weapon, "矛máo (spear)," took its place.

The battle-axe appeared very early, as did the character "戈" representing it, so all characters relating to weaponry and warfare include the form of "戈", such as "戊wu", "戉yue", "戌xu", "戎 rong", "戒jie", "戍shu", "成cheng", and "我wo". In Jiaguwen "戊", "戉", and "戌" are all images of a battle-axe. "戒" shows a defensive position in which a battle-axe is held in both hands, and "戍" means taking guard under a battle-axe. "我" originally represented a serrated weapon, and later it was loaned to indicate "oneself." Other characters relating to weaponry and warfare include "戈", such as "战 zhan (fight)," "武wu (military)," "戚qi (a kind of axe)," and "國(国) guo (country)." It almost goes without saying that "戈" has become a radical indicating weaponry and warfare.

【伐】 In Jiaguwen the character "伐fa (kill)" is an associative-compound character with a clear meaning. The right part is "戈" and the left part is "人", which depicts the barbaric act of a man's head being cut off with the blade of a battle-axe. The original meaning of the character, then, was "chop and kill"; to chop one's head off. Its meaning was extended to "攻打gongda (attach)", "讨伐taofa (crusade against)," and "征伐zhengfa (make punitive expedition)."

Bronze battle-axe (from the Spring and Autumn Period (770-475 BC))

gē

Kaishu

Jiaguwen

Jinwen

Xiaozhuan

Kaishu	Drawings of Character Origin	Jiaguwen	Jinwen	Analysis on Character Form
戊 wù				It is a battle axe with broad blade and long handle.
戉 yuè				It was an axe-shaped weapon or instrument of torture in ancient times and was used to cut people's heads off. Later it was written as "钺yue (battle axe)".
戎 róng				It is the combination of battle-axe and shield, indicating weapons and armies.
戒 jiè				Holding the battle-axe in both hands indicates defense.
戍 shù				A person is under a battle-axe, indicating protection.
戌 xū				It is a battle-axe with a flattened blade and short handle.
成 chéng				Chop down with a broad axe, indicating the finish of killing a person.
我 wǒ				It was a serrated weaponvback in ancient times, and later was adopted as the first-person pronoun.
或 huò				It is town guarded by battle-axes. Later, square borders were added on the surround to form "国guo (country)". The simplified form is "国".

Formation of Character "伐fa (cut down)"
A battle-axe being violently brought down on a person's neck.

Many people were killed in "征伐"; in fact countless soldiers died in major and minor "征伐" throughout China's history. During the Warring States Period (475-221 BC), the Qin State invaded the Zhao State, engaging its forces in Changping, Shanxi. Both sides suffered extensive loss of life. The Qin State's army accounted for 450,000 soldiers of the Zhao State, and half of the Qin's 600,000 soldiers were either killed or wounded. On the battle field, the expressions "尸横遍野shihengbianye (a field littered with corpses)" and "血流漂杵xueliupiaochu (enough bloodshed to float the pestles)", showed this to be one of the most violent and tragic battles in China's history. An estimated 600,000 soldiers are thought to have died on the battlefields of, "长平之, the battle of Changping."

As a verb, "伐" is often used to convey activities such as felling trees; for example "伐木famu (fell trees)," "采伐林木caifa linmu (deforest)," and "砍伐树木kanfa shumu (cut down trees)." However we might still feel slightly squeamish about its macabre original meaning - a person's head being severed with an axe.

【弓】 In Jiaguwen the character "弓gong (bow)" is pictographic, and is an actual drawing of a bow. In Jiaguwen there are two characters of "弓". One is a complete bow, with a curved line on the left representing the bow itself, and a straight line on the left depicting the bowstring. It is also decorated with an additional line, which was where the thread could be tied onto the bow, and then onto the arrow. The arrow could then be easily retrieved after being released. This early type of bow was called "弋(yi)" and was used in fishing and hunting. The other character, "弓" has the same meaning in Jinwen, Xiaozhuan, Lishu and Kaishu. This character contains only the bow, without the bowstring, the bow usually being made of flexible bamboo or wood. Arrows were usually made of bamboo, so the character "箭jian (arrow)" has a form component of "竹(艸)" (bamboo)." In ancient times an arrow was called "矢(shi)". This is also a pictographic character and is written as "↑" in Jiaguwen. Its front end indicates the arrowhead, and the two crossed

fá

伐

Kaishu

Jiaguwen

Jinwen

Xiaozhuan

gōng

弓

Kaishu   Jiaguwen   Jinwen   Xiaozhuan

The Character "射 she (shoot)" in Jinwen
This character quite clearly represents the drawing of a bow.

lines below it represent the feathers at the end of the arrow shaft. Having a heavy arrowhead enables the arrow to travel further and faster, increasing its killing power. The feathers at the end of the arrow balance its shaft, giving it a steadier flight and a more accurate aim.

The ancient Chinese people were very interested in archery. In the time of Confucius, being able to accurately shoot arrows was viewed as one of the "six skills" that everyone who served the state had to master. Bows and arrows played a major role in ancient warfare, and their use would often decide a

Picture of shooting and hunting (primitive rock painting)
The image of shooting and hunting animals frequently appeared in primitive rock paintings.

Picture of birds being shot, from the Warring States Period (475-221 BC) (pattern on the bronze ware)
An archer shooting a flying bird with an arrow attached to a slender thread.

battle. Although bows and arrows are no longer used as weapons, archery remains a popular pastime, and is represented in the Olympic Games.

【盾】 In ancient times the most flexible item in a warrior's armour was a "盾dun (shield)." In combat, a soldier held a battle-axe, spear or sword in one hand, and his shield in the other, so that he could both attack and defend, giving him the maximum strength in battle. The shield played a crucial part in the outcome of a battle, so it became the most representative symbol of defense and attack in ancient times.

In Jiaguwen,"盾dun (shield)" is a pictographic character representing a shield. By the time of Jinwen, it had become an associative-compound character. The upper part is a person and the lower part is a shield, indicating a person holding a shield to defend himself. The earliest shields were made of wood covered with animal hide, and later they were made of metal. Many excavated metal and animal shields still exist today.

There was a popular story in ancient China about a spear and a shield. A man in the Chu State, who was selling weapons, held up his shield and cried out that his shield was the hardest, and that no spear could pierce it. Then he held up his spear and cried out that it was very sharp, and could pierce any shield. A passer-by then asked him, "if I used your spear to pierce your shield, what would happen?" The man thought for a long time but could not answer, and as a result, the phrase came to indicate mutual contradiction.

In ancient times the Chinese people built a huge "shield" – the Great Wall across northern China. For more than 2,000 years it played a significant part in defending the country against invasion by the northern nomadic peoples, safeguarding its

Sunzi Bingfa (Art of War, by Sun Zi):
Sunzi Bingfa is a famous ancient Chinese book on the art of war, and the earliest military text in the world. It was written by Sun Wu, a famous military leader from the Qi State at the end of the Spring and Autumn Period. In the book he provided a detailed explanation of the principles of strategies and tactics, and stressed that in battle one should know the conditions of both oneself and the opposing army. He also said that it was important to focus one's forces on the enemy, and that one should commit to a war once it had begun, but not enter into war without careful thought. *Sunzi Bingfa* indicated that at the time it was written, ancient Chinese military strategies had become extremely sophisticated.

Bronze Shield from the Qin Dynasty

dùn

Kaishu   Jiaguwen   Jinwen   Xiaozhuan

agriculture and the lives of the farmers living in the watershed of the Yellow River. The Great Wall was intended for military defense, rather than attack. It is known as a large "盾" with which ancient China was defended.

The Great Wall; a large "shield" in ancient military defense

Daily Life

The formation of many of the Han characters originated from the everyday lives of the ancient people. Clothing, food, shelter and means of travel are basic necessities for ordinary life, and many Han characters represent these things.

【衣】 "衣yi (clothing)" is a pictographic character. In Jiaguwen, Jinwen and Xiaozhuan, the character clearly represents the ancient outer garment. The upper part is the collar, the lower part is the garment itself, and the empty spaces on either side are the sleeves. Today Chinese people call clothing"衣裳 yishang," but in ancient times it was divided into two words. "衣" referred to the upper outer garment, in the ancient character form "衣" and "裳" (the ancient form being "常") referred to the lower skirt. In ancient times there was a saying that "the upper is "衣" and the lower is "裳'". People used to wear long garments, with wide sleeves and skirts. There was also another type of clothing that combined the upper garment and the skirt, known as "深衣shenyi." Trousers did not appear until later, and were introduced to the Han people by northern nomadic tribes. The nomadic people lived on the plains, and trousers were more practical for horse riding, whereas robes were bulky and awkward. The emergence of trousers marked a revolution in the cultural history of Chinese clothing.

From the time of Jiaguwen - the Shang Dynasty through to the Qing Dynasty - some very colorful types of ancient dress started to appear in China, which are all shown in the form of the character "衣". It seems that the style "衣" dominated Chinese costume for some 3,000 years. When used as a form component, the character "衣" is written as "衤" when on the left or below, and when it is on the right, it remains as "衣". The characters with "衣" as their form components are mostly related to dress, such as "衬chen (underwear)," "衫shan (sleeveless jacket)," "祅

A woman in long skirt from the Song Dynasty (960-1279 AD) This is housed in Jinci Temple, in Taiyuan, Shanxi.

yī

Kaishu

Jiaguwen

Jinwen

Xiaozhuan

Dragon Robe from the Qing
Dynasty (1616 – 1911 AD)

ao (fur garment)," "袍pao (gown)," "裙qun (skirt)," "裘 qiu (fur coat)," and "装zhuang (outfit)." With careful observation, we can see that the component "衤" has evolved from "衣", and that the left-falling and right-falling strokes on the right of the character "衣" have become the two simple dots on the right of "衤".

shí

Kaishu

Jiaguwen

Jinwen

Xiaozhuan

【食】China's imperial rulers set a national policy that the country would be founded on agriculture, based on the notion that "民以食为天 (food is the first necessity of the people)". Today, China is world-famous for its traditional food.

"食shi (food)" is an associative-compound character. In Jiaguwen, the lower part of the character depicts a vessel for cooking food. The two dots at the top indicate that the food is about to boil over, and the triangle at the top represents the cooking pot's lid. Such a vessel was used to cook rice, Chinese sorghum, and millet, so the character "食" when used as a noun, refers particularly to staple foods, although it can also be used for food in general. Some people believe that the triangle at the top of the Jiaguwen character "食" depicts a person's mouth, and that the two dots beneath it represent beads of saliva in anticipation of a good meal. In this interpretation, a person is either looking forward to, or is eating, food, which is a plausible account since the character "食" is related to the action of eating. When used as a noun, it indicates food, such as "主食 zhushi (staple food)" and "冷食lengshi (cold drinks and snacks)," and when used as a verb, it indicates the action of eating, such as the phrases "食肉动物 shirou dongwu (meat-eating animals)" and "废寝忘食 feiqin wangshi (forget food and sleep)." "食" is a radical character, and most characters with "食" as their components are related to "food" or "eating," such as "饭fan (rice)," "饼 bing (cake)," "饮yin (drink)," "饿e (hungry)," and "饱 bao (full)."

Complete Manchu-Han Banquet

The "满汉全席 Manhan Quanxi (complete Manchu-Han banquet)" became popular during the Qing Dynasty (1644-1911), and was a grand Chinese banquet combining the finest and most delicious Manchu and Han dishes. It was an official feast attended jointly by the Manchu and Han people, and contained 108 dishes, and eaten over three days. These consisted of both imperial dishes and local snacks. The Manhan Quanxi remains and important aspect of Chinese food and drink culture.

The character "食" appeared comparatively early. In Jiaguwen it was mainly used to represent "eating a meal," in particular a cooked meal. The culture of Chinese cuisine started with cooked food, a tradition that emerged early in primitive society, when people would eat roasted meat. For example, in the ancient character "炙 (zhi)" the upper part is "肉rou (meat)" and the lower part is "火huo (fire)," which together illustrate meat being roasted over a fire. By the time of Jiaguwen, the culture of food and drink had developed further, and this is exemplified in the characters representing various bronze vessels. For example "鼎ding" was a vessel for boiling meat, "甑(zeng)" was a vessel for steaming food, "簋(gui)" was a container for storing staple foods, "尊zun" was a container for wine, and "爵(jue)" was a cup for drinking wine. All of these can be found in Jiaguwen, and the

Chinese Cuisine:
Chinese food and drink culture has a long history, and its own unique style. After thousands of years of development, various styles of cuisine emerged all across the country. The common expression, "Eight Great Cuisines" refers to Lu (Shandong Cuisine), Chuan (Sichuan Cuisine), Yue (Cantonese Cuisine), Min (Fujian Cuisine), Su (Jiangsu Cuisine, mainly referring to Huaiyang Cuisine), Zhe (Zhejiang Cuisine), Wan (Anhui Cuisine), and Xiang (Hunan Cuisine). There is also another expression, "Four Great Cuisines", which refers to. Lu, Chuan, Huai and Yue. The imperial dishes of Beijing are also very famous, and have long been enjoyed by people all around the world.

character "酉you (wine)" appears in both Jiaguwen and Jinwen. It not only represents the bottle in which wine was contained, but also the "酒jiu (wine)" itself. In the *Shuowen Jiezi*, 67 characters have "酉" as their components, which shows that wine culture has a very a long history in China. There are also many Jiaguwen characters containing the components "食shi (food)," "火huo (fire)," "禾he (ripened grain)," "米mi (rice)," "肉(月)rou (flesh)," "羊yang (sheep)," "酉you (wine)," and "皿min (vessel)." Together these constitute a diverse and varied range of characters relating to food and drink. They not only indicate that Chinese food has a long cultural history, but also reveal one of the most important facts about China; it was, and still is, a largely agricultural country. This adheres to the ancient notion that "民以食为天(Food is the first necessity of the people)."

zhù

住

Kaishu

陣

Xiaozhuan

【住】Chinese architecture has a long history and a distinctive national style, and holds an important position in the world's architectural history. From the footed houses in the southern Hemudu Cultural Ruins and the shallow cave-houses of the northern Banpo Ruins in the remote past, to the Imperial Palace buildings of the Ming and Qing Dynasties, Chinese architecture has a history of some 7,000 years. Ancient Chinese architecture was generally characterized by a wooden structure, wide roof, and planar layout. The

Houses in Beijing

familiar Imperial Palace in Beijing demonstrates these features. These, in turn, were recorded in the Han characters. These characters have form components such as "宀", "穴 xue (cave)," "土 tu (earth)," "木 mu (wood)," "广 guang (wide house)," and "户 hu (house)," and are almost all related to buildings. For example, "宀" illustrates the exterior of a house, with wooden pillars on both sides, and a sharply pointed roof. Characters that indicate dwellings usually have "宀" as their form component, such as "家 jia (home)," "宅 zhai (house)," "安 an (safety)," "宫 gong (palace)," "室 shi (room)," "宿 su (residence)," "寓 yu (residence)," and "宇 yu (eaves)." "广" indicates a wide house with a roof, or a corridor without a wall, and can be found in characters such as "庙 miao (temple)," "fu (mansion)," "ting (court)," "ku (warehouse)," "lang (corridor)" and "dian (store)." These two categories of character refer mostly to buildings with pointed or wide roofs. The characters with "mu (wood)" as their form components usually relate to buildings with a wooden structure, or the use of wooden components in buildings, such as "lou (building)," "zhu (pillar)," and "liang (girder)." The building-related characters that have ""tu (earth)" as their form component, generally illustrate earth and stone structures, such as "qiang (wall)," and "ta (pagoda)." Many further characters are also included in these two categories.

The Six Great Vernacular Dwellings, in China: Civilian houses are the earliest forms of Chinese architecture, and also the most prolific. China covers a vast area and is inhabited by many different ethnic groups. A diverse geographic environment combined with different lifestyles has resulted in houses with many different forms and styles. The so-called "Six Great Traditional Civilian Houses" in China include Siheyuan in Beijing, cave-houses in the northwest, Hui-school civilian houses in Anhui, the mud-hut buildings of Hakka, the bamboo structures of the Tai ethnic group, and the grass Mongolian tents in the north. Of course, the officials' and merchants' grand mansions south of the lower reaches of the Yangtze River, Jin merchants' extensive courtyards in Shanxi, and the courtyards of Xinjiang Uygur, all have distinctive styles of their own.

Hui-School houses in Anhui

Miao houses in Guizhou

Taihe Hall in the Imperial Palace in Beijing
Taihe Hall is an example of typical Chinese architecture, with a wooden structure and a wide roof. The complex of the Imperial Palace is a typical example of a planar layout.

Among the numerous Han characters that indicate buildings, the character "宫 gong (palace)" is notable. It not only indicates a wide roof, but also has the features of a planar layout. If we look directly at the character we can see that the upper "宀" depicts the form of a wide roof, and the two "口" below look like windows. However if we rotate it ninety degrees, it looks like a building plan, with the two "口" indicating many houses. The description of one character "宫" makes use of two angles of observation to show the wide roof and planar layout of ancient Chinese buildings.

【行】 "行 xíng (travel)" is a pictographic character. In Jiaguwen and Jinwen the component characters of "行" look like a crossroads, suggesting that the character's original meaning was "big road." Roads were built for people to walk along, so "行" also means "walk." China is a vast country, with mountains, rivers, lakes, forests and deserts, and the ancient people would often exclaim that "行路难xinglunan (it is difficult to walk)." Short distances could be traveled on foot, but major journeys required boats or carriages. The horse and carriage was the earliest means of long-distance transportation. For example, during the Spring and Autumn period, Confucius visited many princely states to spread his political views, travelling by horse-drawn

Formation of the Character "行 xing (walk)."
"十" is shaped like a major road that people walk along

xíng

行	北	北	北
Kaishu	Jiaguwen	Jinwen	Xiaozhuan

carriages or cattle carts. After uniting China, Emperor Qinshihuang of the Qin Dynasty (221-206 BC), visited many parts of his empire on horse-drawn chariots. Two of these chariots, made of bronze, were unearthed from the mausoleum the Emperor Qinshihuang in Xi'an, and he is believed to have used them to travel around the kingdom. "舟 zhou" means "boat," and is a pictographic character. In Jiaguwen, the character quite clearly represents a small wooden boat. We are certain that boat travel advanced greatly during the Shang Dynasty. When Jian Zhen, a famous monk of the Tang Dynasty (618-907), crossed the eastern sea to preach Buddhism in Japan, he went on a large ship, as did Zheng He, a Ming Dynasty eunuch, when he visited South Asia, West Asia and Africa.

Not everybody, however, used chariots or boats for making long journeys. Xuan Zang, a monk from the Tang Dynasty (618-907), was a famous traveler

Zheng Sailed to the West in a Ship:
Zheng He (1371-1435), originally named Ma Sanbao, was a famous navigator during the Ming Dynasty (1368-1644). In 1405 he commanded a fleet of over 200 ships, carrying a total crew of more than 27,000, and set sail for the West. By 1433, he had undertaken seven voyages, dropped anchor at more than 30 countries, and had been to the east coast of Africa and the shores of the Red Sea. His voyages reflect the very advanced navigational and ship-building skills in China at the time. Zheng He's long navigational voyage was accomplished 50 years earlier, and was grander in scope and accomplishment, than the voyages of some world famous navigators such as Columbus and Vasco da Gama.

Confucius' Long Journey by Carriage

Xuan Zang made a pilgrimage on foot to preach Buddhist scriptures.

who left Xi'an to fetch the Buddhist classics from ancient India. The folk tale *The Pilgrim to the West* was based on his experiences, which were accomplished fully on foot. The same was true of Xu Xiake, a great traveler in the Ming Dynasty, who, like Xuan Zang, traveled tens of thousands of miles on foot. He walked to many places, and recounted his experiences in his book, *Travel Notes by Xu Xiake*.

Cultural Life

【乐】 "乐 yue (music)" is an associative-compound character. The lower part represents wood, and the upper part string. In Jinwen, a character resembling "白" was added to the middle of the string, which looks like a thumb plucking. The whole character resembles an ancient stringed musical instrument. The original meaning of "乐" was in fact "stringed musical instrument." It later became the general term for all musical instruments, and also referred to music itself. In China, music is both loved and frequently performed. The ancient *Shi Jing* (*Classics of Poetry*) recorded more than 70 types of musical instrument, as well as many ancient pieces of music. In ancient times music was closely related to dance and poetry. Every musical composition was accompanied by dance and paintings, such as *Picture of Singing and Dancing*. Because these have lasted to the present day, we can share in the ancient peoples' grand occasions of song and dance. Every poem was sung, and the poems of the *Shi Jing* were all written to be sung; hence the noun "诗歌 shige (poem and song)."

yuè

乐	𐎆	𐎆	𐎆	樂
Kaishu	Jiaguwen	Jinwen	Xiaozhuan	繁体字

139

The musical instruments in the *Night Banquet* by Han Xizai

Because music entertains people, the meaning of "乐" was extended to include joy and happiness, as in "快乐 kuaile (enjoyment)," "欢乐 huanle (happy)," and "乐园 leyuan (land of pleasure)." However in these instances, the character "乐" is not pronounced as "yuè" but as "lè."

In early Chinese art, music, poetry, and dance were closely related. Poems were sung and accompanied with dance.

【舞】 "舞 wu (dance)" was originally a pictographic character. In Jiaguwen the character "舞" looks like a person dancing with a tree branch or oxtail in her hand, and its original meaning was "dance." In Jinwen, two legs were added beneath the character, creating a clearer image of the dancer. The character "舞" had also by then become an associative-compound character. While dancing, people would shout "呜呜(wuwu)!" and the pronunciation of the character "舞", i.e. "wu", might well have originated from this.

Our ancient ancestors would use dance to express their emotions and wishes, especially when trying to communicate with the gods, in hope that they would receive a blessing. At that time, dance was central to magic and sacrifice. The famous "pottery

wǔ

Kaishu   Jiaguwen   Jinwen   Xiaozhuan

Jiaguwen recording people dancing and holding cattle switches to pray for rain

basin painted with dancing patterns," which is 5,000 years old and was discovered in Qinghai Province, has 15 dancers painted onto its inner surface. There were five dancers in each group, holding hands and elegantly stepping in time to a beat. It created a sense of intensity, suggesting that it showed primitive clans celebrating success in hunting, or practicing wizardry. On the rock face of the Huashan Mountain there is a drawing of 9,000 people dancing together at a grand occasion. This provides a lasting record of the sacrificial rituals made to mountain and river gods, and takes us right back to the ancient world. In ancient times, people would dance as part of a dragon worshipping ritual, or when they were praying for rain and favorable weather. Therefore we can be certain that in early times, singing and dancing were not just forms of entertainment. They were connected with the much more important obligations of day-to-day living, and the demands of work.

Pottery Basin Painted with Dancing Patterns (Majiayao Culture)

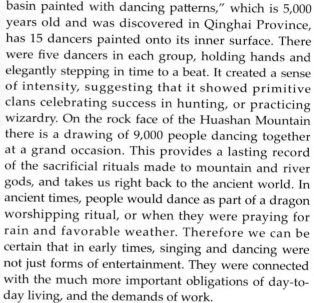

Dancing in the *Night Banquet* by Han Xizai

【册】 Paper-making and print technology were included in the list of the "Four Great Inventions" of ancient Chinese science, so it is not surprising that the earliest printed book came from China. Before books were printed onto paper, they were made from bamboo, which was illustrated in the character "册ce (book)."

"册ce (book)," or "ancient book," is a pictographic character. Before the invention and use of paper, people had to carve characters onto tortoiseshells, animal bones and bronze ware, which came to be known as Jiaguwen and Jinwen respectively. People also wrote characters onto strips of bamboo and bark, but these were comparatively thin, and one leaf usually contained only one line of characters. If people wanted to write lots of characters, they had to bind several wooden strips and bamboo together, using hemp or thread woven from cattle hide. This was represented in the character "册", as in "简册jiance (a book made from cuts of wood or bamboo)." The ancient character "册" resembles such a book. The vertical strokes painted parallel to each other represent the strips of bark, and the rounded horizontal stroke depicts the thread that binds them together. Even today, the Kaishu character "册" still looks like a book made in this way, but has been simplified to represent two strips of bamboo and one thread.

Formation of the Character "典dian (classics)"
A person holding an ancient book in both hands. The drawing is the Jiaguwen character "典".

Many bamboo and wooden strips from the Warring States Period and the Han Dynasty have been discovered. As early as the Jin Dynasty (265-420), several had already been unearthed from the tombs of the Warring States Period. The most famous is the *Zhushu Jinian* (*Chronological Record on Bamboo Book*). The book's name tells us that it is an historical work written on bamboo slips. Later, buried bamboo and wooden pages from the Qin and Han (206 BC-220 AD) Dynasties, were unearthed in

Book made of wooden strips, from the Han Dynasty, unearthed from Juyan in Inner Mongolia

Emperor Qinshihuang of the Qin Dynasty (221 – 206 BC) read books that weighed 60kg because they were painted onto strips of bark.

cè

Kaishu

Jiaguwen

Jinwen

Xiaozhuan

vast quantities. "Slip books" are ancient books, which must have been very heavy. The documents read by Emperor Qinshihuang of the Qin Dynasty (221-206 BC) are believed to have weighed 60kg, and had to be carried to the imperial palace by strong men. They were made of bamboo and bark. A Chinese idiom from the Warring States Period (475-221 BC), "学富五车 xuefu wuche," means "a knowledgeable and well-read person." It is believed that at the time there was a man called Hui Shi, who was extremely knowledgeable and spent a lot of time reading books. Every time he went out, five vehicles would accompany him to carry his books. To be that heavy, they must have been made from wood and bamboo.

The Art of the Han Characters

The artistic nature of the Han characters is demonstrated mainly in calligraphy, fine-art characters and Han character seals. Chinese characters have a particular charm that is unique among the written languages of the world.

Chinese characters originated from drawings. The shapes we see in their square forms are an abstract representation of things in the world around us, such as the sky, earth, mountains, and rivers, and provide a revealing insight into the thought and creativity of the Chinese people. The drawings from which the characters originated were works of great artistic skill, and the characters that resulted from them can be considered works of art in their own right.

The Calligraphic Art of Han Characters

Calligraphy is the scriptural representation of Han characters, and is thought to bring them to life. The Han characters produced in writing cannot be regarded as works of calligraphy, unless they are lively and aesthetic. Calligraphy refers to characters written creatively with vigorous strokes, and is a specific art form. The Han characters are the basis of calligraphy, and in producing it we can reveal, and show appreciation for, their striking artistic quality. The aesthetics of calligraphy actually exceed its practical value, giving it a unique place the world.

Expressing Emotion through Line Art

The beauty of calligraphy lies in the formation of its lines. Han characters are composed of strokes that consist of lines, and the forms of the strokes depend on the movement of their lines, which range from curved to straight. Strokes also utilize spatial structure to illustrate posture, motion, sentiment and meaning. Their lines and forms also evoke different emotions and feelings. In Xiaozhan, Lishu, Kaishu, Xigshu, and Caoshu, the characters' strokes and lines became colorful. Different lines create different kinds of beauty; for example Jiaguwen has thin, hard, and straight lines, and its beauty is in its simplicity. Jinwen has thick, heavy and generous lines, and its beauty is in its extravagance. The lines of Xiozhuan are even and rounded, with a curvaceous beauty, and the lines of Lishu are rounded, slender and vigorous, with a wave-like beauty. The lines of Kaishu are neat and wide, and have a solemn beauty, and the lines of Caoshu are lively and vigorous, with an aerial

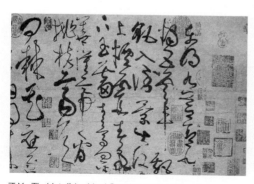

Zi Xu Tie (detail) by Huai Su of the Tang Dynasty

beauty. Xingshu displays a fluent kind of beauty, because its lines are pretty and natural. All are artistically impressive.

Chinese calligraphic art has a very long history. It began some 3,000 years ago, when the people of the Shang Dynasty used a knifepoint to carve Jiaguwen characters onto tortoiseshells and bones. Every dynasty that followed introduced a new style, and produced countless excellent calligraphers. Kaishu and Xingshu are generally seen as the most important styles. For hundreds of thousands of years, people have admired the work of Wang Xizhi from the Eastern Jin Dynasty (317-420), and Yan Zhenqing of the Tang Dynasty (618-907). Wang Xizhi's characters are pretty and fluent, and Yan Zhenqings are vigorous and majestic, resulting in the development of two calligraphic schools. Although the two schools have different styles, they both use calligraphy to express thought and emotion. In doing so they demonstrate that calligraphy is an art that shows the spirit of its creators, rather than just a means of writing.

A Wonderful Artistic Impression

Han characters originated from drawings. The pictographic elements within their square forms represent the forms of everything in the world. Their shapes have a visual quality that inspires the imagination of artists and calligraphers. Phonetic words do not have such qualities. Since ancient times, many artistic works have exploited the pictographic elements of the Han characters, some of which are highly impressionistic.

The character "山 shan (mountain)" has a simple form with only three strokes. However Mi Fu, a great calligrapher from the Song Dynasty (960-1279), made it look strikingly like a high range of mountains. The three peaks rise tall and straight, in powerful, thick strokes, which can be appreciated by anyone looking at them. Mi Fu was also a great artist, who loved mountains and often painted them. His interpretation of the character "山" seems to represent the grandeur and majesty of the mountains in his mind; it was as though he used his brush to express his love for them. There was a saying in ancient

The character "山 shan (mountain)" by Mi Fu

Landscape Painting by Mi Fu

Shangao Yuexiao (High Mountain and Small Moon) by Zhou Qi (modern)

Drawing-like pictographic calligraphic works fully demonstrate the pictographic elements of the Han characters' forms. The appreciation of such works is a visually aesthetic experience.

times that "calligraphy and paintings have the same origin," and that they combined to reflect the natural world. Calligraphy was the art of drawing characters, and drawing was a way of "writing" paintings. Therefore, appreciating a work of calligraphy is said to be similar to admiring a painting of a landscape.

Calligraphers make use of the Han characters' pictographic elements to create pictographic calligraphy. This is an example of a modern work of pictographic calligraphy, "山高月小shangao yuexiao (High Mountain and Small Moon)." On the right we see the characters "山shan (mountain)" and "高gao (high)." The strokes of the character "山" are very thick and actually resemble a high mountain, and the character "高" looks like a house with a sloping roof. Its last stroke extends to the left, and becomes the land. On the left are the characters "月yue (moon)" and "小xiao (small)." "月" is drawn in the shape of a crescent, and "小" is on the lower left, and is smaller. The painting includes both close-up images (the house and land), images at an intermediate distance (the mountains), and images that are far away (the moon, stars, and trees). This brings the scene dimension, and a sense of tranquility. The writer has used the original forms of the pictographic characters to create a striking piece of art.

The pictographic elements of the Han characters provided calligraphers with lots of scope for imagination and artistic creativity. An example is the Caoshu "缚fu (bind)" by Mao Zedong, a modern calligrapher and poet. He drew the character "缚" in one fluid action, so it looks vigorous and lively, and its continuous strokes resemble a large woven net. Using his artistic imagination, he made full use of the form and meaning of the character "缚", painting it boldly

147

Calligraphic Works by Emperor Huizong of the Northern Song Dynasty
(960 -1127 AD)

The Caoshu Character "缚
fu (bind)" by Mao Zedong
(modern)
This Calligrapher used the
character "缚" to weave
a dense and wide net,
creating an artistic effect.

and generously, and in a striking style that everyone can appreciate.

A stroke is produced from the moment the pen touches the paper, to the moment it is raised. Some calligraphers write in one single stroke, a method usually known as "one-stroke calligraphy." The characters 寿(shou, longevity), 福(fu, blessing), 虎(hu, tiger), and 龙(long, dragon), can all be written in one stroke. One-stroke calligraphy looks fluent, lively, and vivid - qualities that many people enjoy.

Special Tools for Calligraphy

Chinese calligraphy is a specific art, and so it employs specific tools, such as the brush pen. Whether we are just appreciating calligraphy, or actually learning it, we must be aware of the tools it employs: the brush pen, ink, stone, and paper. These tools are traditionally known as the "four treasures" in the study of calligraphy. They determine the form, effects, and features of a finished work, and without them, and without expertise in their use, there would be no calligraphy.

Han Characters in Commercial Art

Characters used for commercial purposes also have an artistic design. The upper- and lower-case characters printed in newspapers, magazines, and books, and the variety of typefaces used in advertisements, flyers, postage, and packages, are all commercial characters, designed by artists. Pictographic characters paved the way for the creation of commercial characters, which exhibit some of their visual and decorative features.

Fine-art Characters

Commercial characters have an artistic design and a decorative function. They are different from calligraphy, but still have an artistic nature. Calligraphy expresses its writers' thoughts and feelings through pen and ink, whereas commercial characters are designed to meet the needs of the commercial world, and display the Han characters' artistic nature, with some added decorative effects. Commercial Han characters are different from comparable foreign words, as the latter, often based on the Roman alphabet, do not have a pictographic element. Han characters do have a pictographic element, and their strokes and forms cannot be replicated in any other writing system.

Commercial art based on the Roman alphabet is also very decorative, but is limited to a small number of comparatively simple forms. Because Han characters are pictographic, with a wide range of strokes and forms, they lend themselves more easily to decorative effects.

The character "渔yu (fish)" on Bronze Ware

An inscription of Character "鹿 lu (deer)" on Bronze Ware

The character "龙long (dragon)" on Bronze Ware
This drawing-character "龙long (dragon)", carved onto items of bronze ware, depicts the image of a dragon. It is a vivid, simple, symmetrical and exquisite.

Ancient Public-Art Characters

Since the emergence of the Han characters, many public-art versions have appeared, with the function to decorate, and bring color and interest, to everyday items. Examples of ancient public-art characters include totems, clan badges, bird and insect calligraphy, Xiaozhuan, and characters in the style of the Song Dynasty (960-1279).

Bird and Insect Calligraphy: The most unusual Public-Art Characters in Ancient Times. Some of the most unusual public-art characters in ancient times were those used in bird and insect calligraphy. During the Spring and Autumn Period (770-475), and Warring States Period (475-221 BC), characters decorated with birds, insects, animals, and fish started to appear on the bronze ware of the princely states. This very artistic style of calligraphy expressed the aesthetic interests of the people at the time, and their love for nature. It remained popular for over 300 years. After the Spring and Autumn period and Warring States Period, bird and insect calligraphy gradually disappeared, but it marked a fascinating phase in the history of Chinese art.

Beautiful bird and insect calligraphy (from the Spring and Autumn Period and the Warring States Period

Bird and insect calligraphy was a type of inscription found on bronze ware, which was decorated with the forms of birds, animals, insects and fish. The characters had extended forms and curved lines, and were lively and vivid. They were quite unusual, but very interesting, and much more advanced than the totem characters found on bronze ware from the Shang and Zhou Dynasties.

Xiaozhuan: The most beautiful fine-art characters of ancient times. Of all of the different styles of Han character, Zhuanshu, referring to the Xiaozhuan of the Qin (221-206 BC) and Han (206 BC-220 AD) Dynasties, are considered to have the strongest pictorial quality. Xiaozhuan characters have rounded and artistic strokes, symmetrical forms, and decorative features, and are thought of as examples of fine-art. Xiaozhuan in the Han Dynasty (206 BC-220 AD) had a particularly large-scale colorful forms,

Rubbings of Yishan Keshi (Stone Carving on the Yishan Mountain) by Emperor Qinshihuang of the Qin Dynasty (221 - 206 BC) These Xiaozhuan characters carved onto stone have neat and symmetrical forms with rounded and extended strokes, and show beautiful curvature of calligraphy.

Eaves Tile *Yongfeng Wujiang* (Han Dynasty (206BC - 220AD))

Bronze tiger-shaped tally (Qin Dynasty (221 - 206BC))

and was considered the ultimate in fine-art. Zhuanshu characters are still greatly admired today, and some Chinese people still carve Xiaozhuan name seals. These striking characters can be found on calligraphic scrolls, traditional Chinese paintings, advertisements, newspapers, magazines, buildings, dresses, electrical appliances, stamps, and the national currency.

The basic strokes of Xiaozhuan characters are horizontal, vertical, and curved, with uniform thickness, and appear in rectangular forms with symmetrical and balanced structures. This creates an aesthetic style, making them the most elegant characters. Xiaozhuan has the utmost balance and symmetry, in both its independent and combined characters, and those that are drawn from top to bottom and left to right. During the Qin and Han Dynasties, they were often inscribed onto stone steles, eave tiles, weapons, seals, and bronze coins.

Songtizi Characters: The Most Important Fine-Art Characters of Ancient Times.

Songtizi characters are written in the style of the Song Dynasty (960-1279). After the invention of engraving and wood printing, people began to use knives to engrave the earliest books. A set of square characters, with flat and thin horizontal strokes and thick vertical strokes, became a popular and quick way of writing. These were the Songtizi characters. They represented an improvement on the strokes and structures of Kaishu, and became the standard style for engraving, which at the same time maintained its predecessor's decorative quality. They are also referred to as "songti fine-art characters."

Wood Engraving in the printed book *Zhongwenwang Jishi Shilu (True Records of Prince Zhongwen)*

Hand-written imitation Song-Dynasty Fine-Art Characters
These attractive and elegant imitation Song-Dynasty characters add a unique quality to this passage of handwritten poetry.

沁园春 雪

一九三六年二月

北国风光，千里冰封，

万里雪飘。望长城内外，

余莽莽，大河上下，顿失滔

滔。山舞银蛇，原驰蜡象，

欲与天公试比高。须晴日，

看红装素裹，分外妖娆。

江山如此多娇，引无数

英雄竞折腰。惜秦皇汉武，

略输文采，唐宗宋祖，

风骚。一代天骄，成吉思汗，

只识弯弓射大雕。俱往矣，

数风流人物，还看今朝。

湖笔长锋羊毫

They were perfected during the Ming and Qing Dynasties, and were the genesis of today's finest modern art characters.

Songtizi characters continued to influence those of later generations, and remain in widespread use today. Modern printing presses use adaptations of Songtizi forms, and the style remains an important basis for finely drawn characters. The features of songtizi characters are as follows: the horizontal strokes are flat and thin with a triangular embellishment at the end, the vertical strokes are straight and thick, and the turn of each stroke has a square decoration, which is the natural result of engraving with a reduced cutting. All of the characters, no matter how many strokes they have, must fill identically sized panes. The beauty of the songtizi characters lies in their neatness.

宋体美术字

Printed Song-Dynasty Style Fine-art Characters
Their horizontal strokes are thin, and their vertical strokes are thick and strongly embellished. They look neat, natural, and lively.

宋体美术字

Hand-Written Song-Dynasty Style Fine-Art Characters
Their horizontal strokes are thin and their vertical ones are thick, but their embellishments are inconsistent. The characters look lively, attractive, fresh, and bright.

黑体美术字 Printed Boldface Fine-Art Characters

Modern Han Fine-Art Characters

Modern commercial characters developed from songtizi, and can be printed or hand painted. The two main types of commercial character are songti and boldface, amongst various other styles.

Songti Fine-Art Characters. Many fine-art characters are based on songtizi. They are neat, lively, and aesthetically pleasing, and can be square, oblong or rectangular. Their distinguishing features are their flat and thin horizontal strokes, their straight and thick vertical strokes, and some elaborations. Songtizi has a widespread usage, commonly appearing in books, newspapers and magazines.

Among the songti characters is a type that imitates songtizi. It has longer forms, strokes of an even thickness, horizontal strokes that incline upwards to the right, and is visually very attractive. Imitation songti characters are the prettiest and most elegant, and are often used for writing notations, explanatory notes, subtitles, exhibition plates, and poems.

Boldface Characters. Boldface fine-art characters also developed from songtizi characters. These characters have thickened horizontal strokes, so that the horizontal and vertical strokes

中國藝術　旅游　三角牌
准圆美术体　水柱美术体　粗圆美术体　综艺美术体
长美黑体字　彩云美术体　彩云美术体　细黑美术体

Variant Fine-Art Characters with Various Forms

Hand-Written Variant Fine-Art
Character "术shu (Art)"
These variant fine-art characters with
different forms clearly all developed
from boldface characters.

have the same thickness, and they omit any decorative embellishments. Boldface characters have simple, square forms, look weighty and powerful, and are visually striking. Boldface characters are easy to write and have a wide application. They are often used in headlines, slogans, book titles, and advertisements. Today's colorful modern characters are usually in boldface style.

Variant Fine-art Characters. Variant fine-art characters diverge from the style of songtizi and boldface. Because they are symmetrical, concise, and easy to decorate, many boldface characters have been converted to this style. Variant fine-art characters are vivid, lively, and artistically inspiring, making them popular and widely used.

Variant fine-art characters have a number of forms, which are directly based on songtizi and boldface characters. The Youyuan fine-art style, for example, turns the ends and turns of the boldface strokes into rounded forms, while Changmei boldface results from a combination of songtizi and boldface characters. Several other styles also have altered strokes.

Among the variant fine-art characters, are a kind called variant picture fine-art characters, which have a strong pictorial quality. These make full use of the pictographic elements and inventiveness of the Han characters, resulting in designs and images that are both vivid and striking. As they emphasize the charm of pictographic characters, these are the most popular of the fine-art characters.

"虎hu (tiger)" (decoration on a stamp)
The Jiaguwen character "虎hu (tiger)" was transformed into a beautiful fine-art character, in which the ancient pictographic character "shines through" the modern version.

The Seal Art of the Han Characters

When foreign students studying in China master the language, they are often given a Chinese name seal. Name seals traditionally represent life and soul, and are considered a precious treasure, so people are understandably proud to own them. Seals of Han characters were first used to protect official documents, but they later developed into an exquisite art form in their own right.

Seal Art

Seals carved with Han characters are also known as "made seals." As they are mostly composed of Zhuan characters, they are also known as "Zhuanke" (seal cuttings). They are made from characters being carved onto jade, ivory, animal horns, wood, copper, gold and silver, and a particular artistic style is involved. Back in ancient times, seals were widely used as warrants.

An official seal of the Han Dynasty, *Seal of Empress* (kept in Shaanxi Province Museum)

Official and Private Seals. Ancient Chinese seals had two types of use: official and private. Official seals were a symbol of stature and power, and were carved by emperors or government officials. Private seals were usually the name seals of ordinary people, and were more colorful, and had livelier forms, than the official ones. In ancient times, private seals were called "印yin", "印信yinxin", "印章yinzhang" and "图章tuzhang", and emperors' seals were called "玺xi" or "宝bao." The seals of the Han Dynasty (206 BC-22-AD) represent the best in ancient seal art. Both official and private seals were skillfully carved, and were vivid and simple. They greatly influenced the seal art of later generations.

Qitie Official Seal, from the Han Dynasty (206 BC - 220 AD)

Rubbings of the seal of Prince Chengyang, from the Qin Dynasty

Printed Characters on "Lute." Back in the Qin and Han Dynasties, there was no paper, so documents and letters had to be written on strips of bamboo and wood. Before being delivered, the bamboo or wooden pages would be bound with thread, and the knot would then be sealed with a piece of clay, in order to prevent tampering and unauthorized reading. The clay would then be impressed with an emblem representing the imperial government or the individual author. After it dried out, the clay became very hard, and the three-dimensional impression on its surface was known as "lute." If the lute was broken, it was obvious that someone had opened the document. The seals functioned as warrants to authorize the inspection of the contents. After silk and paper emerged, the lute was no longer used, and the seal was instead pressed directly onto the silk or paper. Archaeologists have discovered that the lute seals were almost all "white character" seals (to be explained in the next passage). The characters on the seals were concave, and after the lute was impressed onto the seal, the characters became raised. The emergence of lute resulted in the development of seals.

The Seals of Literary Scholars. Jade, copper, gold and silver are very hard, and so difficult to make into seals. To begin

Seals on Ancient Paintings
When collecting books, calligraphy and paintings, Chinese people would print their own seals onto them in order to show their ownership. This famous ancient painting *Zhao Ye Bai* by Han Gan, a painter from the Tang Dynasty (618 – 907 AD), is covered in the seals of its previous collectors.

with, professional seal cutters would specially make painters and calligraphers' seals for them. During the Yuan (1206-1368) and Ming (1368-1644) Dynasties, painters and calligraphers discovered types of stone that were comparatively soft and easy to carve onto, and began to personally carve their own seals. They regarded knives as a kind of pen, and fully exploited their artistic abilities on these small stones. After that, seals became bona fide works of art. After completing a work of calligraphy or a painting, the artist would press his or her personal seal onto it, to indicate that it was their own work, expressing their own thoughts, feelings, creativity, and artistic interests. All paintings and works of calligraphy were signed in this way, otherwise they were not considered complete works. Paintings were considered a combination of poetry, calligraphy, painting and seal, and the small red seal had an important role in decorating and balancing the painting.

A white-character seal, *Yu Yan Lou* (玉砚楼), by Huang Yi of the Qing Dynasty

The Beauty of Seals. There are two ways of cutting seals: white-character and red-character. White-character seals (also known as "intaglio character" seals) are directly carved onto the stone, and then pressed onto a red ink pad. The resulting characters are white on a red background (see Yu Yan Lou). Red-character seals (also known as "relief character" seals) are cut around the strokes of the characters, leaving them raised, and when printed they are red (see Jiangnan Buyi).

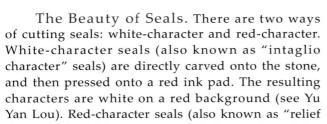

A red-character seal, *Jiangnan Buyi* (江南布衣), by Qi Baishi

The beauty of seals is in their calligraphic style, the skilful way in which they are cut and arranged, the carver's artistry, and the arrangement of the characters' strokes into a small space, as seen in Zhuanshu, Kaishu, and Lishu seals. A single error in any of these aspects could spoil the whole work. In the cutting of the seals, the "soul" of the art is said to lie in the artist's skill, and the seals that are cut with the most skill are the most admired. For example, the red-character seal "江南布衣Jiangnan Buyi" by Qi Baishi, a great modern painter, is both simple and exquisite. The four Zhuanshu characters are inserted into each other and depend on each other, together composing a square form. The carved strokes are both thick and thin, and continuous and separated. They look as though they were completed in one movement - a clear example of the art of skilled carving.

Image Seals. Among the various types of seal are a type known as "image seals," which are carved with images of animals and people. They were first printed onto the lutes of bamboo and wooden strips, as expressions of the creator's interests. They later

Image Seal of a Deer (from the Warring States Period)

Image Seal of a Tiger (from the Han Dynasty)

Chinese Seal Dancing Beijing (Modern Times)

developed into fine works of art that anyone could appreciate. Image seals appeared very early, and became more prevalent during the Spring and Autumn Period and Warring States Period. The people of the Han Dynasty were very fond of image seals, which were colorful, simple, and interesting, and conveyed great spirit. After the Han Dynasty image seals fell out of favor, but they continued to be widely appreciated. They have become popular again in modern times, and the basis of many excellent works. The emblem for the 2008 Olympic Games in Beijing, "Chinese Seal Dancing Beijing," adopted the form of an image seal.

Famous Seals

Many stories about seals have been told throughout Chinese history. Seals that have survived to the present day are seen as cultural and historical artifacts, which have bared witness to historical events.

Gold Seal of King Weinu of the Han Dynasty (from the Eastern Han Dynasty)

Gold Seal, the Seal of the Emperor from the Qing Dynasty

Gold Seal granted to the Dalai Lama of Tibet by the Government of the Qing Dynasty

The Appreciation of Exquisite Seal Art. For thousands of years, calligraphers, painters and seal-cutting enthusiasts have created seals in their own individual styles. The 14 works we see below represent just a fraction of the examples available, which date back to the Ming and Qing Dynasties. All were created by great masters of seal carving.

Calligraphy, fine-art characters and seals represent the best in Han character art, and the Chinese consider them an important part of their cultural heritage. Han character art is still developing today, and new works with original styles and methods continue to appear. Han character art is expected to go on adding character and color to Chinese culture in years to come.

"江流有声，断岸千尺¡± Jiangliu Yousheng, Duan an Qianchi (the rivers flow loudly and rapidly, and their banks are flooded for hundreds of meters either side)", by Deng Shiru of the Qing Dynasty

"柴门深处¡± Chaimen Shenchu (Deep Place from the Gate of Wood)", by He Zhen of the Ming Dynasty

"伯寅藏书¡± Boyin Cangshu (Book Preserved by Boyin)", by Zhao Zhiqian of the Qing Dynasty

"文彭之印¡± Wenpeng Zhiyin (Seal of Wen Peng)", by Wen Peng of the Ming Dynasty

"敬身¡± Jing Shen" by Ding Jing of the Qing Dynasty

梅花无尽藏¡± Meihua Wujin Cang (Preserved by Meihua Wujin)", by Wu Changshuo of the Qing Dynasty

Postscript

I was asked to write this book by the China Intercontinental Press in Beijing.

Written in an accessible style and illustrated with vivid pictures, it is suitable for Chinese readers with a middle-school education and above, and will also appeal to international readers with an intermediate knowledge of the Chinese language, who are interested in Chinese culture. It takes the reader through the ancient yet modern "kingdom" of Chinese characters, helping them to learn and understand the language, and encourages an exchange between Chinese and international culture.

I would like to take this opportunity to express my sincere thanks to all those that supported me in the writing of this book.

Han Jiantang

April 1, 2008, Tianjin.

Appendix:
Chronological Table of the Chinese Dynasties

The Paleolithic Period	c.1,700,000–10,000 years ago
The Neolithic Period	c. 10,000–4,000 years ago
Xia Dynasty	2070–1600 BC
Shang Dynasty	1600—1046 BC
Western Zhou Dynasty	1046–771 BC
Spring and Autumn Period	770–476 BC
Warring States Period	475–221 BC
Qin Dynasty	221–206 BC
Western Han Dynasty	206 BC–AD 25
Eastern Han Dynasty	25–220
Three Kingdoms	220—280
Western Jin Dynasty	265–317
Eastern Jin Dynasty	317–420
Northern and Southern Dynasties	420–589
Sui Dynasty	581—618
Tang Dynasty	618–907
Five Dynasties	907–960
Northern Song Dynasty	960–1127
Southern Song Dynasty	1127–1276
Yuan Dynasty	1276–1368
Ming Dynasty	1368–1644
Qing Dynasty	1644–1911
Republic of China	1912–1949
People's Republic of China	Founded in 1949

Printed in the United States
By Bookmasters